The Harcourt Brace Casebook Series in Literature

Emily Dickinson

A Collection of Poems

THE HARCOURT BRACE CASEBOOK SERIES IN LITERATURE
Series Editors: Laurie G. Kirszner and Stephen R. Mandell

DRAMA
Athol Fugard
"Master Harold" . . . and the boys

William Shakespeare
Hamlet

POETRY
Emily Dickinson
A Collection of Poems

Langston Hughes
A Collection of Poems

SHORT STORIES
Charlotte Perkins Gilman
"The Yellow Wallpaper"

John Updike
"A & P"

Eudora Welty
"A Worn Path"

The Harcourt Brace Casebook Series in Literature
Series Editors: Laurie G. Kirszner and Stephen R. Mandell

Emily Dickinson

A Collection of Poems

Contributing Editor

Marcia Peoples Halio
University of Delaware

Harcourt Brace College Publishers

Fort Worth   Philadelphia   San Diego   New York   Orlando   Austin   San Antonio
Toronto   Montreal   London   Sydney   Tokyo

Publisher:	Earl McPeek
Acquisitions Editors:	Claire Brantley/Julie McBurney
Project Editor:	Andrea Joy Wright
Art Director:	Vicki Whistler
Production Manager:	Linda McMillan

ISBN: 0-15-505487-2
Library of Congress Catalog Card Number: 98-71540

Harcourt Brace College Publishers may provide complimentary instructional aids and supplements or supplement packages to those adopters qualified under our adoption policy. Please contact your sales representative for more information. If as an adopter or potential user you receive supplements you do not need, please return them to your sales representative or send them to: Attn: Returns Department, Troy Warehouse, 465 South Lincoln Drive, Troy, MO 63379.

Address for orders:
Harcourt Brace & Company
6277 Sea Harbor Drive
Orlando, FL 32887-6777
1-800-782-4479

Address for editorial correspondence:
Harcourt Brace College Publishers
301 Commerce Street, Suite 3700
Fort Worth, TX 76102

Web site address:
http://www.hbcollege.com

Printed in the United States of America

8 9 0 1 2 3 4 5 6 7   066   9 8 7 6 5 4 3 2 1

ABOUT THE SERIES

The Harcourt Brace Casebook Series in Literature has its origins in our anthology *Literature: Reading, Reacting, Writing* (Third Edition, 1997), which in turn arose out of our many years of teaching college writing and literature courses. The primary purpose of each Casebook in the series is to offer students a convenient, self-contained reference tool that they can use to complete a research project for an introductory literature course.

In choosing subjects for the Casebooks, we draw on our own experience in the classroom, selecting works of poetry, fiction, and drama that students like to read, discuss, and write about and that teachers like to teach. Unlike other collections of literary criticism aimed at student audiences, The Harcourt Brace Casebook Series in Literature features short stories, groups of poems, or plays (rather than longer works, such as novels) because these are the genres most often taught in college-level Introduction to Literature courses. In selecting particular authors and titles, we focus on those most popular with students and those most accessible to them.

To facilitate student research—and to facilitate instructor supervision of that research—each Casebook contains all the resources students need to produce a documented research paper on a particular work of literature. Every Casebook in the series includes the following elements:

- A comprehensive **introduction** to the work, providing social, historical, and political background. This introduction helps students to understand the work and the author in the context of a particular time and place. In particular, the introduction enables students to appreciate customs, situations, and events that may have contributed to the author's choice of subject matter, emphasis, or style.

- A **headnote,** including birth and death dates of the author; details of the work's first publication and its subsequent publication history, if relevant; details about the author's life; a summary of the author's career; and a list of key published works, with dates of publication.

- The most widely accepted version of the **literary work,** along with the explanatory footnotes students will need to understand unfamiliar terms and concepts or references to people, places, or events.

- **Discussion questions** focusing on themes developed in the work. These questions, designed to stimulate critical thinking and discussion, can also serve as springboards for research projects.

- Several extended **research assignments** related to the literary work. Students may use these assignments exactly as they appear in the Casebook, or students or instructors may modify the assignments to suit their own needs or research interests.

- A diverse collection of traditional and non-traditional **secondary sources,** which may include scholarly articles, reviews, interviews, memoirs, newspaper articles, historical documents, and so on. This resource offers students access to sources they might not turn to on their own—for example, a popular song that inspired a short story, a story that was the original version of a play, a legal document that sheds light on a work's theme, or two different biographies of an author—thus encouraging students to look beyond the obvious or the familiar as they search for ideas. Students may use only these sources, or they may supplement them with sources listed in the Casebook's bibliography (see below).

- An annotated model **student research paper** drawing on several of the Casebook's secondary sources. This paper uses MLA parenthetical documentation and includes a Works Cited list conforming to MLA style.

- A comprehensive **bibliography** of print and electronic sources related to the work. This bibliography offers students an opportunity to move beyond the sources in the Casebook to other sources related to a particular research topic.

- A concise **guide to MLA documentation,** including information on what kinds of information require documentation (and what kinds do not); a full explanation of how to construct parenthetical references and how to place them in a paper; sample parenthetical reference formats for various kinds of sources used in papers about literature; a complete explanation of how to assemble a List of Works Cited, accompanied by sample works cited entries (including formats for documenting electronic sources); and guidelines for using explanatory notes (with examples).

By collecting all this essential information in one convenient place, each volume in The Harcourt Brace Casebook Series in Literature responds to the needs of both students and teachers. For students, the Casebooks offer convenience, referentiality, and portability that make the process of doing research easier. Thus, the Casebooks recognize what students already know: that Introduction to Literature is not their only class and that the literature research paper is not their only assignment. For instructors, the Casebooks offer a rare combination of flexibility and control in the classroom. For example, teachers may choose to assign one Casebook or more than one; thus, they have the option of having all students in a class write about the same work or having different groups of students, or individual students, write about different works. In addition, instructors may ask students to use only the secondary sources collected in the Casebook, thereby controlling students' use of (and acknowledgment of) sources more closely, or they may encourage students to seek both print and electronic sources beyond those included in the Casebook. By building convenience, structure, and flexibility into each volume, we have designed The Harcourt Brace Casebook Series in Literature to suit a wide variety of teaching styles and research interests. The Casebooks have made the research paper an easier project for us and a less stressful one for our students; we hope they will do the same for you.

Laurie G. Kirszner
Stephen R. Mandell
Series Editors

PREFACE

This Casebook was created to help students study the poems of Emily Dickinson and, it is hoped, thereby to see the connections between their lives and the life and work of an unmarried female poet of mid-nineteenth-century New England. The Casebook presents a collection of the poems for discussion and study, along with materials that students can use to write research essays for an introductory literature course.

The Casebook provides a general introduction to the social, political, and literary forces that shaped the time in which Emily Dickinson lived and wrote. To help students see what happens when the private work of a poet is brought to public attention, this introduction briefly discusses the complex publishing history of the poems. Following the introduction, an "About the Author" section provides biographical information.

The Casebook also includes eleven of Dickinson's most famous poems, as well as discussion questions for each poem to help students probe the sometimes complex syntax and cryptic references. At the end of the section on the poetry, general discussion questions and research questions encourage students to go deeper—to read the sources collected in the Casebook or to do further research on the World Wide Web or in the library.

The sources included in this Casebook represent a range of critical work on Dickinson in addition to some primary materials—namely, some of her most interesting and important letters. For many years after the initial publication of her work, literary criticism focused on Dickinson's Puritan heritage or on her unique punctuation, rhymes, and syntax, or her powerful metaphors. In the last fifteen to twenty years, several feminist critics, including Sandra Gilbert, have published interesting work on the effects on Emily Dickinson of being a woman in a highly patriarchal society with prescribed roles for females and little tolerance for individual differences. Judy Jo Small and Richard Sewall also discuss how Emily Dickinson, who often called herself a "songbird," was influenced by music all of her life. The secondary sources are listed and described below:

- Johnson, Thomas H. Ed. *The Letters of Emily Dickinson (Vol. II)*. The Casebook includes eight letters from the Johnson edition: one to Dickinson's friend Mrs. Samuel Bowles, and four to her Preceptor and editor, T. W. Higginson. It also includes three letters written by Mr. Higginson, one to Emily Dickinson and two to his wife describing an interview with Dickinson. The letters reveal Dickinson's state of mind during her most productive period as a poet and express her doubts about the value of her work. They also show her warmth and passion for life and document some of the influences on her work.

- Budick, E. Miller. "The Dangers of the Living Word," from *Emily Dickinson and the Life of Language: A Study in Symbolic Poetics*. An excerpt from a chapter in which Budick discusses the "wild animation and vital energy" of Dickinson's poetic language.

- Farr, Judith. Excerpt from "Art as Life," a chapter in *The Passion of Emily Dickinson*. Farr argues that all of her life Dickinson remained committed to the idea that art must be true to life and love—honest and "fundamental."

- Gilbert, Sandra M. An excerpt from *The Wayward Nun beneath the Hill: Emily Dickinson and the Mysteries of Womanhood*. Gilbert demonstrates how Dickinson used the materials of daily life—bread, puddings, dresses, plum cakes—as inspirations for her poetry. By becoming a "magician of the ordinary," Dickinson transformed her routine, domesticated existence into extraordinary texts.

- Sewall, Richard B. "Early Friendships" from *The Life of Emily Dickinson*. Sewall gives a vivid account of Dickinson's early friendships and their effects on her life, especially as they influenced her "musicality."

- Small, Judy Jo. An excerpt from the chapter "A Musical Aesthetic," from her book *Positive as Sound*. Small argues that, influenced by the Romantics, Dickinson thought of poetry "as music, as song, and she expresses her revisionary intent in musical terms."

- Tate, Allen. "Emily Dickinson," from *Collected Essays*. In this essay, originally published in 1932, Tate sums up Dickinson's place in literature, comparing her with Emerson, Hawthorne, John Donne, Shakespeare, Tennyson, and Arnold, calling her a great poet. It is important to note that when Tate's essay was written, many of Dickinson's finest poems had not yet been published.

• Wells, Henry W. "Romantic Sensibility," from his book *Introduction to Emily Dickinson*. In this essay, published in 1947, Wells argues that although Dickinson cannot be grouped with any of the Romantic poets because of the Puritan, Calvinist influence in her work, she was, nevertheless, touched deeply by the new "insensibility" of the Romantic movement.

In addition to the secondary sources listed above, the Casebook also includes a student paper written by Rachel Lavery. Because of her double major in music and literature, Rachel is uniquely qualified to write this paper about the relationships between the "musicality" of Dickinson's poems and interpretations given to her work by twentieth-century composers. Although Rachel's paper illustrates imaginative use of source material and correct MLA documentation style and format, it was chosen mainly because it illustrates how a student can use a personal approach to assigned material and thus make the material her own. Throughout the paper the ideas of the critics supplement and support Rachel's own ideas, and as a result her own voice dominates the discussion.

The Casebook concludes with an extensive bibliography of print and electronic sources on Emily Dickinson.

Acknowledgments

No project as ambitious as the Casebook series happens without the help of many talented and dedicated people. First, I would like to thank Laurie Kirszner and Stephen Mandell, who developed the Casebook idea in their text *Literature: Reading, Reacting, Writing*. Next, I would like to thank the people who worked with me on the Emily Dickinson Casebook: the production manager, Linda McMillan; the art director, Vicki Whistler; and the project editor, Andrea Wright. Finally, I would like to thank Michael Rosenberg, who suggested turning the Casebooks into a series, and without whose enthusiastic help and support this project would never have come into being.

CONTENTS

An introduction to the social, historical and political influences
during Emily Dickinson's lifetime.

Introduction

Telling the Truth "Slant"

"Tell all the Truth but tell it slant"
#1129
Emily Dickinson (1830–86)

Although she wrote over 1,700 poems and is considered one of America's major poets, Emily Dickinson published fewer than a dozen poems during her lifetime. Her highly idiosyncratic work is filled with questions, visions, and images that were disturbing to nineteenth century New England editors accustomed to safe, conventional verse. Dickinson questioned everything: her Puritan heritage, human relationships, love, the senses, the meaning of time, life, death, nature, and eternity. Because she did not avoid harsh realities, her observations often made readers uncomfortable. She knew that life holds pain and loneliness and that few people are ever fully understood. She saw that it is necessary to tell the truth, but that, if we tell it, we risk repercussions. She knew that we all suffer loss and frustration, but she maintained a lively wit and sense of humor that sustained her when she needed them.

Never afraid to take a risk, Emily Dickinson nourished her mind and soul from many sources. Building on her Puritan heritage and formal education in the arts and sciences, she read sentimental romantic novels, popular psychology and theology, and fugitive slave narratives. In addition, she read Hawthorne, Emerson, Thoreau, Longfellow, William Cullen Bryant, Shakespeare, the Brownings, the Brontës, George Eliot, Sir Thomas Browne, and the Bible.[1] Her reading sustained her through a lifetime of hard work and independent thought.

When Dickinson was born in 1830, New England, like much of the rest of the fledgling United States, was in a period of transition leading to the Civil War, and was moving from a largely agrarian society of shared

---

[1] For a description list of Dickinson's library, see Richard B. Sewall, "Books and Reading," *The Life of Emily Dickinson*, New York: Farrar, Straus and Giroux, 1974. Chapter 28.

beliefs to an industrialized urban society that gave more value to individual thought. When she was a child, Puritanism[2] had largely loosened its adherence to absolute truths that often made ordinary New England life seem like a dramatic struggle, a contest of heroic proportions between good and evil. Nevertheless, the tenets of Puritanism had become something of an unconscious discipline, passed from generation to generation. No longer did sinners "quake in the hands of an angry God" as Puritan minister Jonathan Edwards preached—except perhaps during revival meetings. By the nineteenth century, Puritanism had become a way of looking at the world, stressing work, duty, and social responsibility. As Dickinson sat with her family in the pew in Connecticut Valley Congregational Church, listening to sermons, she rejected the doctrine that preached the utter depravity of man, but she did learn the discipline of an intellectual life that prompted her to question everything she saw, heard, or felt. She absorbed the vocabulary and symbols of Calvinist[3] belief that in later years she transformed into personal metaphors in her poetry. Words central to Calvinist theology—*seal, covenant, ordinance* and *promise*—appear often in her poetry, and the theme of an individual's relationship to God, especially as it concerns immortality, troubled her throughout her lifetime.

The daughter of Edward Dickinson, a Harvard-trained lawyer who was treasurer of Amherst College and grandson of one of its founders, Emily was surrounded from an early age by books and intellectual discussions. Although her mother "did not care for thought" (Johnson and Ward 260) she did not seem to discourage Emily from having an intellectual life of her own. At age ten, Emily was enrolled at Amherst Academy, a coeducational institution founded in the New England tradition of educating future ministers, and she studied there until she was 17. She studied the arts, English literature, rhetoric, philosophy, Latin, French, German, history, geography, classics, and the Bible. In addition, she had an excellent grounding in the sciences, mathematics, geology, botany, natural history, physiology and astronomy. From her scientific training, she learned habits of close observation such as note keeping and looking at specific, concrete details—a discipline of mind that was to prove useful to her as she gathered specimens of

---

[2] The militant Christianity of early New England settlers that advocated strict religious discipline and simplification of the ceremonies and beliefs of the Church of England.

[3] An ultra-conservative form of Christianity that emphasized the sinfulness of man, the omnipotence of God, the supremacy of the scriptures, the need to be born again, the salvation of the "Elect" (those predetermined to be saved), and a strict moral code.

flowers for her botany collection, and observations of nature for her poetry, throughout her lifetime. This scientific training also encouraged her skepticism and gave her the ability to absorb the revolution in the physical sciences that nineteenth-century America was to witness. The habit of close observation also strengthened her writing. Throughout her poems, Dickinson never loses her appreciation for detail: a flower, a bird, a fly, a butterfly, fresh berries, the sea, words, trains, children, lightning—nothing escapes her notice. And seeing makes her aware of life as a *process,* of the passage of time, and of change.

Because she did not oversimplify experience, Dickinson saw many paradoxes: the apparent contradiction between work as duty and work as joy; the human desire for a peaceful death and for a rich life; the desire for solitude and the need for companionship; the desire for success and for anonymity; the desire for cool introspection and for heated passion; the desire for activity and for repose; the desire for intoxication and for sobriety; the desire for unquestioning belief and for a clear, skeptical mind. Always, Dickinson struggled to find the correct path for herself. All around she saw conflict and transformation and felt herself different from the people in her community. Even so, she managed, through reading and writing, to find a community of her own.

A writer of extreme sensibilities and sensitivities, Dickinson balanced her naive idealism against the cynicism that came with the experience of loss and pain. Many times she suffered the loss of a loved one or disappointment over her inability to publish her writing or the perceived slight of a friend, but she remained open to life and its possibilities. Surrounded by people who were not as inquisitive, she turned for companionship to books, where she found inspiration, education, and competition. Through reading, she met others who had vividly expressed their experience of life. Sometimes she used an idea from her reading in her own work until it grew surer, stronger, bolder. In this way, she used her writing to sharpen her perceptions, to see more clearly the transforming process of nature and to understand the metamorphosis and rebirth of the human mind tempered by new ways of looking at the world.

With great effort, she managed to reconcile her religious inheritance with her experience, taking the basic vocabulary of Calvinism and redefining it to fit her view of life. She balanced her need for daydreaming with the need for discipline, and the need for service to others with her need for service to herself. As she matured as a writer, she employed strong metaphors that expressed her visions in startling and sometimes cryptic ways. Forced to censor thoughts and feelings that were at odds with church doctrine, she knew early on that she must come to the truth *slant*—that is, through indirection and metaphor, revealing some while concealing much. In her poetry, she communicated through riddles and paradoxes, vivid images and mysterious comments, and by the use of mysterious dashes, unusual capitalization, irregular rhythms, and *slant rhymes*—that is, words that don't quite rhyme, but almost do. As a result, her poetry grew economical, but filled with tension and wit.

For nearly all of Dickinson's life, her father was the shaping influence in the house. Daily, he led morning prayers for servants and members of the family, and he was suspicious of books other than the Bible. As she lived under her father's roof, Emily struggled to find her own way while catering to his idiosyncratic whims (for example, he would eat only bread that she baked). At his death in 1874, Dickinson wrote to her friend T. W. Higginson, a critic and editor on the *Atlantic Monthly*, that her father's "heart was pure and terrible" (Johnson and Ward, L 418). Her mother, Emily Norcross Dickinson, seems to have had little influence on her life; ineffectual and distant from her children, she was a pleasant shadow to her overpowering husband.

In her childhood, Dickinson sat for hours listening to long sermons in the church pew with her father and mother, and with her older brother Austin and her younger sister Lavinia ("Vinnie"). It's easy to suppose that in these pews she must have allowed her mind to wander to the fields and meadows that surrounded the town; she must have daydreamed about the birds and insects, about the flowers of the countryside in which she played with her cousins and siblings. She stored up these childhood memories that would sustain her later when, as an adult, she retreated to her bedroom to write for more than twenty years. In the church pews, she also absorbed the rhythm of the hymns, three- or four-beat meters that influenced her poetry for many years.

In 1847, at age 17, Emily attended Mt. Holyoke Female Seminary (later to become Mt. Holyoke College) and roomed with her cousin, Emily Norcross. While at Mt. Holyoke, she attended a fundamentalist Calvinist revival meeting where she was pressured to stand and declare herself a Christian. Emily Dickinson (like several other girls) refused to stand. She did not return to Mount Holyoke the following year, remaining instead in Amherst, where she experienced the most socially active period of her life.

During her twenties, she occupied her time with ordinary chores such as bread-making and her days were governed by frugality, practicality, work, duty, concentration, and outward conventionality—all approved of in conservative New England. In the midst of this intellectual famine, she developed a reading circle that nourished her mind. Students from Amherst College gathered at the Dickinson family home with Emily, her sister Vinnie, and her brother Austin, who smuggled books into the house. With her friends and siblings, Dickinson read her New England compatriots Hawthorne, Emerson, Thoreau, Longfellow, and William Cullen Bryant, as well as classics of English literature and the Bible. She also took extended trips to Boston and Washington.

By the time she was in her thirties, however, Emily had retreated to her room and seldom, if ever, left the house and garden. Her younger sister Lavinia knew that Emily was very bright, and encouraged her to write. Emily wrote reams of letters to friends and family—even to her brother Austin and his wife (Sister Sue), who lived next door with their three children. Although her choice to live as a recluse meant confinement, it also gave her a kind of freedom. Dressed in white, mysteriously appearing at the window of the second story of the house to lower baskets of cookies and cakes for the children of the neighborhood, Emily became the ghostly spirit of the town. Some thought she was eccentric, even disturbed. Perhaps she deliberately created this eccentric persona. Had she been more conventional, she would have been expected to spend her life doing the things that maiden ladies did in New England in the 1850s and 1860s—caring for the sick and the elderly, for example. Because she was considered strange, people largely left her alone, giving her the time and energy to do as she wished. Although she cooked for parties and baked bread for her father, Emily was free to stay up late at night to write and think and explore the world of her mind, surrounded by her "friends"—the writers whose works she adored. Her favorite writers had created characters who opposed the expected norms of the societies in which they lived, and these characters spoke to Emily. She also continued to explore the world of perceptions, keeping detailed notes on flies, snakes, flowers, the slant of light on a winter afternoon; nothing escaped her notice.

Like her New England ancestors, Dickinson lived with the presence of death—of crops, of animals, of people. She was aware of the forces of nature and of nature as an enemy (in many of her poems the symbol of Nature is Death). Knowing the value of hard work, stamina, shrewdness, and practicality, she wasted nothing, writing her poems on the backs of envelopes, or scraps of paper as she worked alone in her room, late at night. Considering work a duty for the glory of God, she kept diaries, evaluating her conduct during the day, realizing that the burden of proof of her Christianity was on her.

As she wrote, Dickinson reacted strongly to the unpoetic atmosphere in which she lived. Whicher acknowledges this atmosphere when he writes that by the 1850s:

> [s]everal generations of looking at little but the bare, unpoetized facts of pioneer experience [had] transformed the New Englander into a small man of affairs, with an abnormally developed bump of ingenuity for dealing with practical issues. He had no time to waste on poetry, which indeed he was right in thinking had lost connection with what vitally concerned him. The Bible, the almanac, and the newspaper comprised his stapler reading (158–59).

Dickinson saw ample evidence of the effects of this trend in her father, who was too busy with politics[4] and local and national affairs for poetry and intellectual discussions. During her youth every American had vaguely expected to rise in the world, but during her lifetime the closing of the frontier and the spread of industrialization changed all that. Outside of quiet Amherst frustration, dissatisfaction, and criticism replaced the old optimism. By 1850, great fortunes had been made in the rum-for-slaves trade and in the milling industries. The Gilded Age of gaudy consumption had begun, but according to Allen Tate, "culture, in the truest sense, was disappearing. . . . The new order flattened out [the eclectic excitement] in a common experience. . . . It exalted more and more the personal, the unique in the interior sense. . . . The nineteenth-century New Englander, lacking a genuine religious center (like the Puritans), began to be a social conformist" (200). Redemption was replaced by respectability, external uniformity, spiritual sterility. Ralph Waldo Emerson became "the prophet of a piratical industrialism" (Tate 200), preaching his gospel that man is greater than any idea. Although Dickinson wrote during the Gilded Age, she was not affected by it: her mind had been shaped during the three expansive decades before the Civil War (1830–60).

In addition to the political and social changes taking place in the United States in the mid-nineteenth century, the 1850s were also an extraordinary period in the history of American literature, but Dickinson did not seem to notice. According to Conrad Aiken, she hardly mentions the tremendous literary events which took place during her youth. When she was seventeen, Ralph Waldo Emerson was at the height of his career, living nearby and

---

[4] During this period, Dickinson's father served in the state legislature and the U.S. Congress.

promoting his revolutionary ideas of Transcendentalism.[5] When she was twenty, Nathaniel Hawthorne, another New England neighbor, published *The Scarlet Letter;* the next year, he published *The House of the Seven Gables,* and Herman Melville published *Moby Dick.* In 1849, Edgar Allan Poe died, and the first edition of his collected poems was published the year after. Around this same time, Thoreau's *Walden* and Walt Whitman's *Leaves of Grass* appeared. This was indeed the full flowering of American literature, but Dickinson seems to have been influenced by little of the period except Emerson's preaching of mystical individualism (Aiken 11–12). According to Tate, her "ideas were embedded in her character, not taken from the latest tract" (207). He compares her to Shakespeare: "The world order is assimilated, in Miss Dickinson, as medievalism was in Shakespeare, to the poetic vision; it is brought down from abstraction to personal sensibility" (209). Tate sees her as "the last surprising bloom—the November witch-hazel blossom—of New England's flowering time . . . somewhere between Hawthorne and Emerson philosophically. . ." (204).

During the 1860s, Dickinson corresponded with several editors, especially Thomas Higginson of the *Atlantic Monthly* (see the letters to and from Higginson in the Sources section of this Casebook) and Samuel Bowles of *The Springfield Daily Republican*, but she succeeded in publishing only a few poems. When she got advice from her correspondents, it was often bad: many critics wanted her to become more conventional, to standardize her highly individual punctuation, capitalization and spelling, and to conform to expected usage. Fortunately, Dickinson resisted this advice and stuck to her own instincts, maintaining her highly original voice and style.

In her period of greatest creativity (1861–62), she wrote hundreds of poems. Although her output of poetry declined in her later years, she continued to write eloquent letters. For the last twenty years of her life, Dickinson worked alone in her room, surrounded by her beloved books and by portraits of some of her favorite writers: French novelist George Sand, English novelist George Eliot (author of *Middlemarch*), and poet Elizabeth Barrett Browning—all women writers who succeeded in a man's world. By keeping to her room, Emily avoided both the stifling conventionality of a small Puritan town and the responsibility of social obligations.

---

[5] The belief that individuals can experience God firsthand; therefore, there is no need for the forms and ceremonies of any church.

Beginning with her father's death in 1874, Dickinson suffered a number of serious personal losses. In 1875 her mother was paralyzed by a stroke; she and Vinnie cared for her for eight years until her death in 1882. During this period, Emily became close to her mother, who had never been a strong figure in her life. In the year of her mother's death, her friend and long-time correspondent, the Rev. Charles Wadsworth of Philadelphia, also died. Although he had visited Emily at Amherst only twice in twenty years, they had maintained a lively exchange of letters. Some critics say that he was the love of her life, and the inspiration for the famous letters to the "Master," a series of mysterious love letters written to and about an unidentified figure who is worshipped and adored. During the late 1870s and early 1880s, Dickinson had an admirer, Judge Otis Phillips Lord of Salem, with whom she maintained a close relationship until his death in 1884. The most severe blow during this period was the death of her nephew, Gilbert, the son of Austin and Sue; in 1883, he died at age 8 of typhoid fever: some say Emily never really recovered from this loss. Finally, in 1885 she experienced the loss of her life-long friend and correspondent, Helen Hunt Jackson, author of *Romola,* who had urged Dickinson many times to seek publication more aggressively. In 1878 Jackson had arranged secretly for the publication of one of Dickinson's most famous poems, "Success is counted sweetest" (see p. 16). This poem was met with critical acclaim; in fact, some critics attributed it to Emerson.

After Dickinson's death in 1886, her sister Vinnie discovered bureau drawers full of poems bound together by the poet into little books, or fascicles. Astounded at her sister's productivity, she divided the poems, giving some to Austin's wife Sue, Dickinson's most trusted friend and critic, and some to Mabel Loomis Todd, who had been Austin's lover for thirteen years. This act created a seventy-year battle for control of the poems that lasted until the death of Sue's daughter, Martha Dickinson Bianchi, and Mabel's daughter, Millicent Todd Bingham, when the poems were acquired by Harvard University.

Publication History

Mabel Loomis Todd was the first to publish a large number of Dickinson's poems. In 1890, she coedited, along with *Atlantic Monthly* editor

T. W. Higginson, a collection of over 100 poems. This collection contained some of the most famous poems, but others were missing because they were in the possession of Austin and Sue. In the tradition of the time, Todd and Higginson "cleaned up" the poems—eliminating many of the special characteristics that make Dickinson's work unique. They added titles, substituted more conventional language for her highly personal and individual use of words, and changed some of the rhymes to conform to expected norms. In 1945, Millicent Todd Bingham (daughter of Mabel), published the more than 600 poems held by her mother, many of them unpublished before. She also wrote three biographical studies of the Dickinson family, but because of her mother's troubled relationship to the Dickinsons, she was an unreliable biographer. In 1956, Mrs. Bingham gave the Dickinson poems and papers inherited from her mother to Amherst College. In 1968, she left her own and her parents' papers to Yale.

Between 1914 and 1973, Martha Dickinson Bianchi, daughter of Susan and Austin, brought out eight volumes of Dickinson's poetry. Like Mabel Todd and T. W. Higginson, she too, "cleaned them up." In 1950, the poems in her possession were acquired by an intermediary who gave them to Harvard University. The editing barbarism continued throughout many editions of the poems until the Thomas H. Johnson Harvard edition of 1955 restored the original mechanics and word choice. The Johnson edition, which gives the publishing and manuscript history for each of the more than 1,700 poems, is considered basic to Dickinson scholarship. (A new edition by R. W. Franklin is in preparation.)

For thirty years after the publication of the Johnson edition, Dickinson criticism centered largely on two issues: the influence of Puritanism on her poetry and her mystical imagery and idiosyncratic punctuation, diction, and versification. Since the 1980s, feminist scholars such as Judith Farr, Sandra Gilbert, and Susan Gubar have focused on Dickinson as a woman writer (see the bibliography entry Feminist Criticism on page 113), attributing her use of cryptic language and indirection to nineteenth century New England pressures on women to speak softly and timidly. Certainly, the early poetry is self-absorbed, but as Dickinson matured, her themes became more universal. Hundreds of hand-written pages from her most productive period (1861–62) are filled with her large handwriting and show a mind teeming with impressions from the sensory world and insights from personal experience. When she leaves her early self-absorption and enters a wider universe of thought and perception, her poems often achieve greatness, and her art is deliberate, growing increasingly complex. In the later poems, Dickinson uses slant rhymes and indirect syntax, inverting the expected word order to suggest the complexity of her thought and the difficulty of coming to terms with her themes.

In the final analysis, Dickinson's work endures because she told the truth of the human journey as she saw it. She shared her joys, her pains, and her perceptions, treating her readers as mature adults who could participate fully in life's symphony. Like all writers, Emily Dickinson rearranged the details of experience, emphasizing some, turning others into metaphor, but she always remained true to the knowledge of the human heart.

For more information on the life of Emily Dickinson, see the bibliography entry "Biographies" on page 109. The most authoritative Dickinson biography is *The Life of Emily Dickinson,* by Richard B. Sewall, (New York: Farrar, Straus and Giroux, 1974).

WORKS CONSULTED

Aiken, Conrad. *Collected Criticism of Conrad Aiken: A Reviewer's ABC.* Greenwich: Meridan, 1958.

Farr, Judith, ed. *Emily Dickinson: A Collection of Critical Essays.* Englewood Cliffs: Prentice-Hall, 1996.

———. *The Passion of Emily Dickinson.* Cambridge: Harvard UP, 1992.

Johnson, Thomas H. *Emily Dickinson: An Interpretive Biography.* Cambridge: Harvard UP, 1955.

Johnson, Thomas H., ed. *The Poems of Emily Dickinson: Including Variant Readings Critically Compared with All Known Manuscripts.* Cambridge: Belknap-Harvard UP, 1955.

Johnson, Thomas H. and Ward, Theodora, eds. *The Letters of Emily Dickinson.* Cambridge: Harvard UP, 1958.

Longsworth, Polly. *Emily Dickinson: Her Letter to the World.* New York: Crowell, 1965.

Sewall, Richard B. *The Life of Emily Dickinson.* 3 vols. New York: Farrar, 1974.

Tate, Allen. *Collected Essays.* Denver: Swallow, 1932. Scribner's, 1938.

Whicher, George Frisbie. *This Was a Poet: A Critical Biography of Emily Dickinson.* NY: Scribner's, 1938. Introd. Richard B. Sewall. Hamden: Shoe String, 1980.

Literature

About the Author

EMILY DICKINSON (1830–86) was born in Amherst, Massachusetts to a socially prominent family. Her father, Edward Dickinson, was a lawyer, a judge, and a member of Congress, and was also treasurer of Amherst College and one of its founders. He had high expectations for his children, expecting a strict adherence to the moral code of their Puritan heritage. Emily Dickinson's mother, Emily Norcross Dickinson, was an obedient wife with conventional views, who provided little companionship for her sensitive, questioning daughter. Emily was close to her older brother Austin and her younger sister Lavinia, who fidgeted with her during long sermons and enjoyed romps in the surrounding countryside when the opportunity rose.

In her youth, Emily attended Amherst Academy: at age 17 she matriculated at Mt. Holyoke Female Seminary (later to become Mt. Holyoke College) where she refused to stand and be counted as a born-again Christian. After her freshman year, Emily did not return to Mt. Holyoke; instead, she remained in Amherst to help her sister Lavinia with the housework, especially baking bread, which she enjoyed. Eventually, as her friends married or moved away, Emily retreated more and more to her room to write. Her poems record her struggle to come to terms with her sensitive romantic tendencies and her New England Puritan heritage. In addition to poetry, she wrote thousands of passionate, searching letters, many to her brother Austin's wife Sue, who lived next door.

During her most creative period in the 1860s, she tried to publish some of her poems but succeeded in publishing only a few. In fact, her work went largely unnoticed until her death in 1886, when her sister Lavinia discovered some 1,700 poems tucked away in Emily's bureau drawers. Beginning in 1890, several editions of the poems appeared, but the editors often changed Emily's highly individual words and punctuation, regularizing them to conform to conventional usage and thus altering the poems significantly. In 1955, Harvard University published the Thomas H. Johnson edition of the poems, which restored the original mechanics and word choice. This is the definitive edition that details the publishing history and shows various versions of certain poems. Several editions of her poetry are also available on the World Wide Web (see the bibliography for a list of sites).

To study Dickinson's poetry is to see the growth of a writer. She writes of pain and struggle from a unique perspective and forces her readers to see life in new ways. Because of her startling honesty, she leaves us with some of the most memorable poems in American literature.

The Poems

Following are eleven of Dickinson's most famous poems, chosen because they touch on her major themes and illustrate her development as a writer. A study of these poems can give you a basic introduction to the work of Emily Dickinson. As you gain an appreciation for the richness of her work, you may also wish to consult major collections of her poetry such as the 1955 T. H. Johnson Harvard edition. The text of the poems and the numbering are from the T. H. Johnson edition.

#67

Success is counted sweetest
By those who ne'er succeed.
To comprehend a nectar[1]
Requires sorest need.

Not one of all the purple Host
Who took the Flag today
Can tell the definition
So clear of Victory

As he defeated—dying—
On whose forbidden ear
The distant strains of triumph
Burst agonized and clear!

---

[1] Nectar: in Greek mythology, the drink of the gods

Discussion Questions

1. What is Dickinson's attitude toward success? Write a one- or two-sentence paraphrase of the poem.

2. There are two central images in the poem through which Dickinson tries to show (rather than tell) what success means. The first is the image of the victor; the second, the vanquished. How does Dickinson paint the picture of the victor? What kinds of details does she use to describe the vanquished? How does she appeal to our senses of sight and sound?

#214

I taste a liquor never brewed—
From Tankards scooped in Pearl—
Not all the Frankfort Berries[2]
Yield such an Alcohol!

Inebriate of Air—am I—
and Debauchee of Dew—
Reeling—thro endless summer days—
From inns of Molten Blue—

When "Landlords" turn the drunken Bee
Out of the Foxglove's door—
When Butterflies—renounce their "drams"—
I shall but drink the more!

Till Seraphs swing their snowy Hats—
And Saints—to windows run—
To see the little Tippler
From Manzanilla come!

---

[2] The 1890 Higginson and Todd edition *Poems* changed "Frankfort Berries" to "vats upon the Rhine."

Discussion Questions

1. This poem puzzles some readers. In fact, early editors changed some of the wording so that it would be less ambiguous. To help you understand the message—the mood that Dickinson was trying to convey—paraphrase the poem.

2. When the 1890 version of the poem was published, the editors made two important changes: they changed "Frankfort Berries" to "vats upon the Rhine" and "From Manzanilla come" to "Leaning against the sun." In your opinion, what is gained and what is lost by these changes? Read the lines aloud to hear the difference in the sound. Which wording creates more vivid images in the mind of the reader?

#249

Wild Nights—Wild Nights!
Were I with thee
Wild Nights should be Our luxury!

Futile—the Winds—
To a Heart in port—
Done with the Compass—
Done with the Chart!

Rowing in Eden—
Ah, the Sea!
Might I but moor—Tonight—
In Thee!

Discussion Questions

1. This poem seems straightforward: it is, of course, a love poem—sexual and reasonably explicit. To understand it fully, read it aloud. Note the rhythm of rowing. Note the sound of the *w*'s. Try paraphrasing the poem in a paragraph. Is it possible to express all the images and emotions in prose? If not, why not? What can poetry do here that prose cannot? For

example, how does Dickinson use words such as *compass, chart, port,* and *Eden* to create a sexually explicit image?

2. Why do you think the editors were worried about publishing this poem in 1891? Do you think readers today would be shocked by such a poem? What has changed in the intellectual and social environment in the last century to cause a different reaction from readers?

#288

I'm Nobody! Who are you?
Are you—Nobody—too?
Then there's a pair of us!
Don't tell! They'd banish us—you know!

How dreary—to be—Somebody!
How public—like a Frog—
To tell your name—the livelong June—
To an admiring Bog!³

Discussion Questions

1. In this poem, Dickinson seems to be writing to a very special audience for a special purpose. To whom do you think this poem is written? Why do you think she wrote it?

2. What is the effect of the capital letters? What is the effect of the dashes? What would be lost if they were edited out?

3. Compare Dickinson's opening line "I'm Nobody! Who are you?" to Charles Mackay's⁴ "Who would be a Somebody?— Nobody am I." Which is more effective? Why? To answer these questions, read the lines aloud, and think about both content and sound. Which line better engages the reader? Why?

---

³ Bog: marsh or swamp

⁴ Charles Mackay was the author of a poem entitled "Little Nobody," which was published in the *Springfield Daily Republican* 23 January 1858. Dickinson probably read his poem.

#303

The Soul selects her own Society—
Then—shuts the Door—
To her divine Majority—
Present no more—

Unmoved—she notes the Chariots—pausing—
At her low Gate—
Unmoved—an Emperor be kneeling
Upon her Mat—

I've known her—from an ample nation—
Choose One—
Then—close the Valves of her attention—
Like Stone—

Discussion Questions

1. In this poem Dickinson uses simple language to make an abstract con-
   cept—the soul—concrete. In doing so, she creates a vivid image. To
   what is the Soul being compared? "Souls," at least in the traditional sense,
   do not have doors to shut, gates to bar access, mats to kneel upon, and
   valves to close. Why is this simple diction so powerful?

2. What is Dickinson saying in this poem about her own personality, her
   own way of choosing people to love? Do you understand her idea of
   "shutting the Door" of the Soul to new people? Why might someone
   want to do that?

#435

Much Madness is divinest Sense—
To a discerning Eye—
Much Sense—the starkest Madness—
'Tis the Majority
In this, as All, prevail—

Assent—and you are sane—
Demur—you're straightway dangerous—
And handled with a Chain—

Discussion Questions

1. Dickinson's style is characterized by spare language: she uses nouns and verbs but very few adjectives. Examine the language in this poem. What are the key words? Which words have strong emotional associations? Which are concrete?

2. What is Dickinson saying here about "Madness"? Can the word have more than one meaning? Can one be "mad" if one is simply different from others? Who are the "Majority" she speaks of? What is the meaning of *assent* and *demur*? Why do you think she chose those particular words?

#441

This is my letter to the World
That never wrote to Me—
The simple News that Nature told—
With tender Majesty

Her Message is committed
To Hands I cannot see
For love of Her—Sweet—countrymen—
Judge tenderly—of Me

Discussion Questions

1. You may find Dickinson's use of the pronoun *Her* in the second stanza puzzling: perhaps it refers to Nature in the first stanza, since Nature is often viewed as female. What do you think?

2. In what sense are Dickinson's poems "letters to the World"? Examine several of the poems in this Casebook and try to determine the audience

for each one. Does the audience change, or is there a constant "World" to which she writes? Use examples from the poems to support your opinion.

❖ ❖ ❖

#465

I heard a Fly buzz—when I died—
The Stillness in the Room
Was like the Stillness in the Air—
Between the Heaves of Storm—

The Eyes around—had wrung them dry—
And Breaths were gathering firm
For that last Onset—when the King
Be witnessed—in the Room—

I willed my Keepsakes—Signed away
What portion of me be
Assignable—and then it was
There interposed a Fly—

With Blue—uncertain stumbling Buzz—
Between the light—and me—
And then the Windows failed—and then
I could not see to see—

Discussion Questions

1. Do you think Dickinson actually saw a fly in a room where someone was dying? Does it matter? Why does she use such a common insect? Why not an unusual one? How does her use of the fly help her reach her readers?

2. Dickinson has sometimes been called a "morbid" poet because several of her poems deal with death (see, for example, #712, "Because I could not stop for Death"). Do you find her morbid? Why, or why not? Given the circumstances of her life, why might Dickinson have written so much about death?

#585

I like to see it lap the Miles—
And lick the Valleys up—
And stop to feed itself at Tanks—
And then—prodigious step

Around a Pile of Mountains—
And supercilious peer
In Shanties—by the sides of Roads—
And then a Quarry pare

To fit its sides
And crawl between
Complaining all the while
In horrid—hooting stanza
Then chase itself down Hill—

And neigh like Boanerges—[5]
Then—prompter than a Star
Stop—docile and omnipotent
At its own stable door—

Discussion Questions

1. Dickinson's train is not a machine, but an animate creature, lapping,
   licking, stopping, stepping, peering, fitting, crawling, complaining,
   chasing, neighing, and finally, stopping at its "stable door" (like a horse).
   At a literal level, what is Dickinson describing in this poem? Write a
   one- or two-sentence paraphrase.

2. The strong action verbs and the concrete nouns (along with a few very
   vivid adjectives) create the image of a train passing through the valleys,

---

[5] The name given by Jesus to the Apostles John and James, who were known as "sons of
thunder." Used to indicate a loud-voiced preacher or orator. Dickinson must have heard
several such preachers in New England churches and at revival meetings.

mountains, and hills surrounding Amherst. List the verbs, nouns, and adjectives and analyze Dickinson's choices. Why do they work so well?

3. Look at the syntax in the poem. Why, for example, does Dickinson interrupt her lines with inverted phrases such as "prodigious step" (instead of "stepping prodigiously") and "supercilious peer" (instead of "peering superciliously"). Why, in the last stanza, does she interrupt the flow of her words with "docile and omnipotent"? Why doesn't she say, for example, "Stop at its own stable door, docile and omnipotent"?

#712

Because I could not stop for Death—
He kindly stopped for me—
The Carriage held but just Ourselves—
And Immortality.

We slowly drove—He knew no haste
And I had put away
My labor and my leisure too,
For His Civility—

We passed the School, where Children strove
At Recess—in the Ring—
We passed the Fields of Gazing Grain—
We passed the Setting Sun—

Or rather—He passed Us—
The Dews drew quivering and chill—
For only Gossamer, my Gown—
My Tippet[6]—only Tulle—

We passed before a House that seemed
A Swelling of the Ground—
The Roof was scarcely visible—
The Cornice—in the Ground—

---

6 Tippet: short cape or scarf

Since then—'tis Centuries—and yet
Feels shorter than the Day
I first surmised the Horses' Heads
Were toward Eternity—

Discussion Questions

1. Who is the driver? How do we know he is courteous and considerate?
   What do the passengers in the carriage see on the ride?

2. In this poem, Dickinson uses an extended metaphor—a carriage ride—
   to discuss a journey we are all destined to take someday. Why do you
   think she chose this metaphor? Why did she personify death? How does
   the use of a metaphor and the personification of death help to make an
   abstract concept concrete?

#1129

Tell all the Truth but tell it slant—
Success in Circuit lies
Too bright for our infirm Delight
The Truth's superb surprise
As Lightning to the Children eased
With explanation kind
The Truth must dazzle gradually
Or every man be blind—

Discussion Questions

1. The meaning of this poem resides in the word *slant*. What does Dickin-
   son mean by this word? Some people think she means that writers should
   "slant" the truth by altering it, as when a biased narrator tells a story. Do
   you agree? Paraphrase the poem in a sentence or two. What is Dickinson's
   attitude toward telling the truth? Why does she think it is important?
   How should it be told?

2. Written at the end of her most creative period, this poem sums up Dickinson's attitude toward writing: that it is a powerful tool that, like the Lightning in line 5, can enlighten the mind. List the words in the poem that show Dickinson's attitude toward truth-telling. How powerful is the truth to Dickinson?

Text of poems reproduced by permission from *The Poems of Emily Dickinson,* Thomas H. Johnson, ed. Cambridge: The Belknap Press of Harvard University Press, Copyright © 1951, 1955, 1983.

<h1 style="text-align:center">General Discussion Questions on the Poetry</h1>

1. Based on the eleven poems included in this casebook, what general statements can you make about Dickinson as a poet? What are her major themes? What are her stylistic techniques?

2. Do you think Dickinson's work will continue to be popular for the next one hundred years? Why or why not?

3. How is Dickinson similar to other poets you have studied? How is she different? Give examples from the work of other poets to support your opinions.

4. Of the eleven poems in this casebook, which one seems most powerful to you? Why?

5. If you have enjoyed the poems in this volume, investigate some of Dickinson's other work: "There's a certain Slant of light" (#258)[7]; "After great pain, a formal feeling comes—" (#341); "A narrow fellow in the Grass" (#986); "I never saw a Moor—" (#1052); and "My life closed twice before its close—" (#1732). Imagine that you were going to prepare an edition of selected Dickinson poems. Which ones would you include, and why?

---

[7]   Numbers refer to the T. H. Johnson Harvard edition of Dickinson's poetry, 1955.

Research Questions

1. Many critics have noted the importance of Dickinson's New England Puritan heritage on her poetry. Others have noted her romantic sensibilities. Using several of the sources included in this casebook, and others that you may find in your library, do some background reading on the major influences on Dickinson's poetry. Then enter the debate yourself. Which side do you stand on? What do you think is the most important influence on Dickinson's work—her New England Puritan heritage, or her reading of Shakespeare, Emerson, the Brownings, and Keats? To build your case, cite references from the critics as well as from the poetry itself.

2. When Dickinson's poetry was first published in 1890, four years after her death, it was heavily edited by Mabel Loomis Todd and Henry W. Higginson to make the rhymes more regular and the wording and syntax clear. This editing trend continued until the T. H. Johnson edition of 1955. Examine several poems as they have appeared in different editions.[8] Do you think this editing was justified or not? Use evidence from the critics, letters, and poems to support your opinion.

3. Critic Allen Tate has said Emily Dickinson's life is her work. In what ways is this statement true? In what ways is it false? To research this question, first do some background reading in some of the biographical sources included in this casebook, as well as others in your library. Once you have formed some impressions, focus on a particular aspect of her life, such as her friendship with her sister-in-law Sue or her love of nature, and use the source material as well as the poetry and letters to take a stand.

4. In recent years, feminist critics such as Suzanne Juhasz, Vivian Pollak, and Sandra Gilbert have studied the ways in which Dickinson's poetry is influenced by her perception of her role as a woman in mid-nineteenth century New England. To examine this issue, first do some background reading, starting with the sources provided in this casebook and the letters and poems of Dickinson. Then, consult other sources in your library or

---

[8] Several editions of Dickinson's poetry can be found on the World Wide Web. For a rich collection, visit the Alabaster site at the University of Virginia (*www.engl.virginia.edu/~ennc491/alabaster/text/INTRO/html*).

online, for example the www.sappho.com site on the World Wide Web
or the University of Maryland site on women's issues at www.inform.
umd.edu/EdRes/Topic/WomensStudies/. What are the main issues
outlined by feminist critics? Choose one of these issues and consider
it carefully, studying the critics, Dickinson's letters, and the poems
themselves. To what extent is Dickinson's work influenced by her
gender?

5. In his play *The Belle of Amherst*, William Luce used the letters and
poems of Emily Dickinson to create a two-hour monologue depicting
scenes from her life. Read the play or watch the videotaped performance
starring Julie Harris as Emily Dickinson. Using the poems, letters, and
biographical criticism in this casebook and elsewhere, critically assess the
play. Does the play accurately reflect Dickinson's life? What is gained by
compressing the action of her life into a two-hour monologue? What
is lost?

6. In several letters and poems, Dickinson refers to herself as a "songbird."
In a letter to a friend upon the death of a family member, for example,
Dickinson wrote: "Let Emily sing for you because she cannot pray." In
1949–50, Aaron Copland set several of Dickinson's poems to music,
including "Because I could not stop for Death"[9] (see page 24). Listen
to a recording of the Copland music or examine the score listed in the
Music section of the bibliography. What is the effect of the music? In
what ways is Dickinson a "musical" poet? Use recordings, critics, her
letters, and her poems to support your conclusion.

7. Is Dickinson "didactic"? That is, does she tell us what to think and feel?
Does she try to impose moral values on her readers? According to Allen
Tate, she is not; others disagree. What do you think? Using evidence from
the poems, the Luce play, and critics, build a case of your own.

8. Many critics (e.g., Sewall and Tate) have expressed opinions about the
meaning of the white dress Dickinson always wore. Read the critics'
opinions, the poetry, and the letters, and then build an argument of your
own. Why do *you* think she wore white? Cite evidence from your reading
to support your opinion.

9. Some critics have compared Dickinson to her contemporary New En-
gland authors: philosopher Ralph Waldo Emerson; novelist Nathaniel

---

[9] Copland used the title "The Chariot" given in the Bianchi and Hampson edition.

Hawthorne; novelist Henry James, who published during the 1870s and 80s; and Jonathan Edwards, a poet of the Puritan era whose work she could not have read, since it was published after her death. Still others have compared her to the seventeenth-century English metaphysical poets such as John Donne and George Herbert. Choose one of these writers and do a comparison of your own. How is Dickinson's work similar to the author you have chosen? How is it different? Use some of the sources from the casebook to clarify your reading of the poems or to debate the opinions expressed by the critics.

10. Some critics have said that Dickinson was morbidly fascinated by death; others disagree. What do you think? How do contemporary poets write about death? Choose some twentieth-century poets— such as Sylvia Plath, A. E. Housman, Theodore Roethke, Adrienne Rich, Nikki Giovanni, Rita Dove, Judith Ortiz Cofer, Wendy Rose, Joy Harjo, or William Carlos Williams—and examine their treatment of this theme. Compare one or two of their poems to Dickinson's poems about death, and try to account for the differences.

11. Research some of the other poets of Dickinson's period—for example, Henry Wadsworth Longfellow, James Russell Lowell, Oliver Wendell Holmes, John Greenleaf Whittier, or Walt Whitman— and examine some of their themes. How is Dickinson like them? How is she different?

12. One hundred years after her death, Dickinson's poetry still lives. Why do you think this is so? Is she merely an eccentric regional poet defined by her New England heritage who happened to become famous because her work was discovered in a drawer after her death? Or does her work achieve universal quality? Using evidence from the poems, the letters, the critics, or the sites on the World Wide Web, examine the reasons for her continued popularity.

Secondary Sources

Each of the sources in this section* offers insights into Emily Dickinson's poetry that can help you understand, enjoy, and write about the poems. The sources included in this section range from letters written by or to Dickinson during a period of great struggle in her life to articles and book chapters on Dickinson's reading, her family, her Puritan heritage, her Romantic tendencies, and her unusual rhythm and metaphors. You may use these sources to generate ideas that could be developed into a paper, or you may find materials that support a paper topic you have already chosen. After you have read these sources, you can use the bibliography at the back of this book to locate further resources pertaining to Dickinson's life and work. Remember to document any words or ideas that you borrow from these and any other sources. (See the appendix for more information about proper documentation format.)

THOMAS H. JOHNSON AND THEODORA WARD, EDS.

From The Letters of Emily Dickinson
(1958)

235

To Mrs. Samuel Bowles   *about August 1861*

Mary.

    I do not know of you, a long while—I remember you—several times— I wish I knew if you kept me? The Dust like the Mosquito, buzzes round my faith.

---

* Note that several of the sources do not use the documentation style recommended by the Modern Language Association and explained in the Appendix.

We are all human—Mary—until we are divine—and to some of us—
that is far off, and to some [of] us—near as the lady, ringing at the door—
perhaps that's what alarms—I say I will go myself—I cross the river—and
climb the fence—now I am at the gate—Mary—now I am in the hall—
now I am looking your heart in the Eye!

Did it wait for me—Did it go with the Company? Cruel Company—
who have the stocks—and farms—and creeds—and *it* has just it's heart!
I hope you are glad—Mary—no pebble in the Brook—today—no film
on noon—

I can think how you look—You cant think how I look—I've got more
freckles, since you saw me—playing with the schoolboys—then I pare the
"Juneating" to make the pie—and get my fingers "tanned."

Summer went very fast—she got as far as the woman from the Hill—
who brings the Blueberry—and that is a long way—I shall have no winter
this year—on account of the soldiers—Since I cannot weave Blankets, or
Boots—I thought it best to omit the season—Shall present a "Memorial"
to God—when the Maples turn—

Can I rely on your "name"?

How is your garden—Mary? Are the Pinks true—and the Sweet Wil-
liams faithful? I've got a Geranium like a Sultana—and when the Hum-
ming birds come down—Geranium and I shut our eyes—and go far
away—

Ask "Meme"—if I shall catch her a Butterfly with a vest like a Turk? I
will—if she will build him a House in her "Morning—Glory." Vinnie would
send her love, but she put on a white frock, and went to meet tomorrow—
a few minutes ago. Mother would send her love—but she is in the "Eave
spout," sweeping up a leaf, that blew in, last November. Austin would send
his—but he dont live here—now—He married—and went East.

I brought my own—myself, to you and Mr Bowles. Please remember
me, because I remember you—Always.

> My River runs to thee—
> Blue Sea! Wilt welcome me?
> My River waits reply—
> Oh Sea—look graciously—
> I'll fetch thee Brooks
> From spotted nooks—
> *Say*—Sea
>   Take *Me!*

260

To T. W. Higginson   *15 April 1862*

Mr Higginson,

Are you too deeply occupied to say if my Verse is alive?

The Mind is so near itself—it cannot see, distinctly—and I have none to ask—

Should you think it breathed—and had you the leisure to tell me, I should feel quick gratitude—

If I make the mistake—that you dared to tell me—would give me sincerer honor—toward you—

I enclose my name—asking you, if you please—Sir—to tell me what is true?

That you will not betray me—it is needless to ask—since Honor is it's own pawn—

In place of a signature, ED enclosed a card (in its own envelope) on which she wrote her name. This first letter to Higginson, which begins a correspondence that lasted until the month of her death, she wrote because she had just read his "Letter to a Young Contributor," the lead article in the *Atlantic Monthly* for April, offering practical advice to beginning writers. She also enclosed four poems: "Safe in their Alabaster Chambers," "The nearest Dream recedes unrealized," "We play at Paste," and "I'll tell you how the Sun rose." When Higginson first published the letter (in the first publication named above), he introduced it by saying: "On April 16, 1862, I took from the post office in Worcester, Mass., where I was then living, the following letter."

261

To T. W. Higginson   *25 April 1862*

Mr Higginson,

Your kindness claimed earlier gratitude—but I was ill—and write today, from my pillow.

Thank you for the surgery—it was not so painful as I supposed. I bring you others—as you ask—though they might not differ—

While my thought is undressed—I can make the distinction, but when I put them in the Gown—they look alike, and numb.

You asked how old I was? I made no verse—but one or two—until this winter—Sir—

I had a terror—since September—I could tell to none—and so I sing, as the Boy does by the Burying Ground—because I am afraid—You inquire my Books—For Poets—I have Keats—and Mr and Mrs Browning. For Prose—Mr Ruskin—Sir Thomas Browne—and the Revelations. I went to school—but in your manner of the phrase—had no education. When a little Girl, I had a friend, who taught me Immortality—but venturing too near, himself—he never returned—Soon after, my Tutor, died—and for several years, my Lexicon—was my only companion—Then I found one more—but he was not contented I be his scholar—so he left the Land.

You ask of my Companions Hills—Sir—and the Sundown—and a Dog—large as myself, that my Father bought me—They are better than Beings—because they know—but do not tell—and the noise in the Pool, at Noon—excels my Piano. I have a Brother and Sister—My Mother does not care for thought—and Father, too busy with his Briefs—to notice what we do—He buys me many Books—but begs me not to read them—because he fears they joggle the Mind. They are religious—except me—and address an Eclipse, every morning—whom they call their "Father." But I fear my story fatigues you—I would like to learn—Could you tell me to grow—or is it unconveyed—like Melody—or Witchcraft?

You speak of Mr Whitman—I never read his Book—but was told that he was disgraceful—

I read Miss Prescott's "Circumstance," but it followed me, in the Dark—so I avoided her—

Two Editors of Journals came to my Father's House, this winter—and asked me for my Mind—and when I asked them "Why," they said I was penurious—and they, would use it for the World—

I could not weigh myself—Myself—

My size felt small—to me—I read your Chapters in the Atlantic—and experienced honor for you—I was sure you would not reject a confiding question—

Is this—Sir—what you asked me to tell you?

Your friend,
E—Dickinson.

Higginson says in his *Atlantic Monthly* article introducing the letter (cited above) that the enclosed poems were two: "Your riches taught me poverty," and "A bird came down the walk." But the evidence after study of the folds in the letters and poems suggest that he was in error. The enclosures seem to have been: "There came a Day at Summer's full," "Of all the Sounds despatched abroad," and "South Winds jostle them." Harriet Prescott Spofford's "Circumstance" was published in the *Atlantic Monthly* for May 1860. Higginson's "Letter to a Young Contributor" quotes Ruskin and cites Sir Thomas Browne for vigor of style. The article's comment on "what a delicious prolonged perplexity it is to cut and contrive a decent *clothing of words* . . ." may explain ED's phrase "While my thought is undressed." The friend who taught her "Immortality" has generally been thought to be Benjamin Franklin Newton. The two editors who recently had asked her for her mind may have been Bowles and Holland.

Though ED frequently refers to the Brownings, she never again mentions Ruskin or Browne, and Keats but twice (see letters no. 1018 and 1034).

265

To T. W. Higginson   *7 June 1862*

Dear friend,

Your letter gave no Drunkenness, because I tasted Rum before— Domingo comes but once—yet I have had few pleasures so deep as your opinion, and if I tried to thank you, my tears would block my tongue—

My dying Tutor told me that he would like to live till I had been a poet, but Death was much of Mob as I could master—then—And when far afterward—a sudden light on Orchards, or a new fashion in the wind troubled my attention—I felt a palsy, here—the Verses just relieve—

Your second letter surprised me, and for a moment, swung—I had not supposed it. Your first—gave no dishonor, because the True—are not ashamed—I thanked you for your justice—but could not drop the Bells whose jingling cooled my Tramp—Perhaps the Balm, seemed better, because you bled me, first.

I smile when you suggest that I delay "to publish"—that being foreign to my thought, as Firmament to Fin—

If fame belonged to me, I could not escape her—if she did not, the longest day would pass me on the chase—and the approbation of my Dog, would forsake me—then—My Barefoot-Rank is better—

You think my gait "spasmodic"—I am in danger—Sir—

You think me "uncontrolled"—I have no Tribunal.

Would you have time to be the "friend" you should think I need? I have a little shape—it would not crowd your Desk—nor make much Racket as the Mouse, that dents your Galleries—

If I might bring you what I do—not so frequent to trouble you—and ask you if I told it clear—'twould be control, to me—

The Sailor cannot see the North—but knows the Needle can—

The "hand you stretch me in the Dark," I put mine in, and turn away—I have no Saxon, now—

> As if I asked a common Alms,
> And in my wondering hand
> A Stranger pressed a Kingdom,
> And I, bewildered, stand—
> As if I asked the Orient
> Had it for me a Morn—
> And it should lift it's purple Dikes,
> And shatter me with Dawn!

But, will you be my Preceptor, Mr Higginson?

Your friend

E Dickinson—

The phrase "I have no Saxon" means "Language fails me": see *Poems* (1955) 197, where in poem no. 276 she offers "English language" as her alternative for "Saxon." She enclosed no poems in this letter.

268

To T. W. Higginson   *July 1862*

Could you believe me—without? I had no portrait, now, but am small, like the Wren, and my Hair is bold, like the Chestnut Bur—and my eyes, like the Sherry in the Glass, that the Guest leaves—Would this do just as well?

It often alarms Father—He says Death might occur, and he has Molds of all the rest—but has no Mold of me, but I noticed the Quick wore off those things, in a few days, and forestall the dishonor—You will think no caprice of me—

You said "Dark." I know the Butterfly—and the Lizard—and the Orchis—

Are not those *your* Countrymen?

I am happy to be your scholar, and will deserve the kindness, I cannot repay.

If you truly consent, I recite, now—

Will you tell me my fault, frankly as to yourself, for I had rather wince, than die. Men do not call the surgeon, to commend—the Bone, but to set it, Sir, and fracture within, is more critical. And for this, Preceptor, I shall bring you—Obedience—the Blossom from my Garden, and every gratitude I know. Perhaps you smile at me. I could not stop for that—My Business is Circumference—An ignorance, not of Customs, but if caught with the Dawn—or the Sunset see me—Myself the only Kangaroo among the Beauty, Sir, if you please, it afflicts me, and I thought that instruction would take it away.

Because you have much business, beside the growth of me—you will appoint, yourself, how often I shall come—without your inconvenience. And if at any time—you regret you received me, or I prove a different fabric to that you supposed—you must banish me—

When I state myself, as the Representative of the Verse—it does not mean—me—but a supposed person. You are true, about the "perfection." Today, makes Yesterday mean.

You spoke of Pippa Passes—I never heard anybody speak of Pippa Passes—before.

You see my posture is benighted.

To thank you, baffles me. Are you perfectly powerful? Had I a pleasure you had not, I could delight to bring it.

Your Scholar

"Pippa Passes," the first of the series in Browning's "Bells and Pomegranates," had been published in 1841. The letter enclosed four poems: "Of Tribulation these are they," "Your Riches taught me poverty," "Some keep the Sabbath going to Church," and "Success is counted sweetest."

271

To T. W. Higginson   *August 1862*

Dear friend—

Are these more orderly? I thank you for the Truth—

I had no Monarch in my life, and cannot rule myself, and when I try to organize—my little Force explodes—and leaves me bare and charred—

I think you called me "Wayward." Will you help me improve?

I suppose the pride that stops the Breath, in the Core of Woods, is not of Ourself—

You say I confess the little mistake, and omit the large—Because I can see Orthography—but the Ignorance out of sight—is my Preceptor's charge—

Of "shunning Men and Women"—they talk of Hallowed things, aloud—and embarrass my Dog—He and I dont object to them, if they'll

exist their side. I think Carl[o] would please you—He is dumb, and brave—
I think you would like the Chestnut Tree, I met in my walk. It hit my no-
tice suddenly—and I thought the Skies were in Blossom—

Then there's a noiseless noise in the Orchard—that I let persons hear—
You told me in one letter, you could not come to see me, "now," and I made
no answer, not because I had none, but did not think myself the price that
you should come so far—

I do not ask so large a pleasure, lest you might deny me—
You say "Beyond your knowledge." You would not jest with me, because
I believe you—but Preceptor—you cannot mean it? All men say "What" to
me, but I thought it a fashion—

When much in the Woods as a little Girl, I was told that the Snake
would bite me, that I might pick a poisonous flower, or Goblins kidnap me,
but I went along and met no one but Angels, who were far shyer of me, than
I could be of them, so I hav'nt that confidence in fraud which many exercise.

I shall observe your precept—though I dont understand it, always.
I marked a line in One Verse—because I met it after I made it—and
never consciously touch a paint, mixed by another person—

I do not let go it, because it is mine.
Have you the portrait of Mrs Browning? Persons sent me three—If you
had none, will you have mine?

Your Scholar—

With this letter ED enclosed two poems: "Before I got my Eye put
out," and "I cannot dance upon my Toes."

330a

From T. W. Higginson

Sometimes I take out your letters & verses, dear friend, and when I feel
their strange power, it is not strange that I find it hard to write & that long
months pass. I have the greatest desire to see you, always feeling that per-
haps if I could once take you by the hand I might be something to you; but
till then you only enshroud yourself in this fiery mist & I cannot reach you,
but only rejoice in the rare sparkles of light. Every year I think that I will
contrive somehow to go to Amherst & see you: but that is hard, for I often
am obliged to go away for lecturing, &c & rarely can go for pleasure. I would
gladly go to Boston, at any practicable time, to meet you. I am always the
same toward you, & never relax my interest in what you send to me. I should
like to hear from you very often, but feel always timid lest what I *write*

should be badly aimed & miss that fine edge of thought which you bear. It would be so easy, I fear, to miss you. Still, you see, I try. I think if I could once see you & know that you are real, I might fare better. It brought you nearer e[ven] to know that you had an actual [?] uncle, though I can hardly fancy [any?] two beings less alike than yo[u] [&?] him. But I have not seen him [for] several years, though I have seen [a lady] who once knew you, but could [not] tell me much.

It is hard [for me] to understand how you can live s[o alo]ne, with thoughts of such a [quali]ty coming up in you & even the companionship of your dog withdrawn. Yet it isolates one anywhere to think beyond a certain point or have such luminous flashes as come to you—so perhaps the place does not make much difference.

You must come down to Boston sometimes? All ladies do. I wonder if it would be possible to lure you [to] the meetings on the 3^d Monday of every month at Mrs. [Sa]rgent's 13 Chestnut St. at 10 am—when somebody reads [a] paper & others talk or listen. Next Monday Mr. Emerson [rea]ds & then at 3½ P.M. there is a meeting of the Woman's [Cl]ub at 3 Tremont Place, where I read a paper on the [Gre]ek goddesses. That would be a good time for you to come [alth]ough I should still rather have you come on some [da]y when I shall not be so much taken up—for my object is to see you, more than to entertain you. I shall be in Boston also during anniversary week, June 25* & 28,—or will the Musical Festival in June tempt you down. You see I am in earnest. Or don't you need sea air in summer. Write & tell me something in prose or verse, & I will be less fastidious in future & willing to write clumsy things, rather than none.

Ever your friend
[signature cut out]

*There is an extra meeting at Mrs. Sargent's that day & Mr. Weiss reads an essay. I have a right to invite you & you can merely ring & walk in.

342a

From T. W. Higginson
to his wife

I shan't sit up tonight to write you all about E.D. dearest but if you had read Mrs. Stoddard's novels you could understand a house where each member runs his or her own selves. Yet I only saw her.

A large county lawyer's house, brown brick, with great trees & a garden—I sent up my card. A parlor dark & cool & stiffish, a few books &

engraving & an open piano—Malbone & O D [Out Door] Papers among other books.

A step like a pattering child's in entry & in glided a little plain woman with two smooth bands of reddish hair & a face a little like Belle Dove's; not plainer—with no good feature—in a very plain & exquisitely clean white pique & a blue net worsted shawl. She came to me with two day lilies which she put in a sort of childlike way into my hand & said "These are my intro-duction" in a soft frightened breathless childlike voice—& added under her breath Forgive me if I am frightened; I never see strangers & hardly know what I say—but she talked soon & thenceforward continuously—& defer-entially—sometimes stopping to ask me to talk instead of her—but readily recommencing. Manner between Angie Tilton & Mr. Alcott—but thor-oughly ingenuous & simple which they are not & saying many things which you would have thought foolish & I wise—& some things you wd. hv. liked. I add a few over the page.

This is a lovely place, at least the view Hills everywhere, hardly moun-tains. I saw Dr. Stearns the Pres't of College—but the janitor cd. not be found to show me into the building I may try again tomorrow. I called on Mrs. Banfield & saw her five children—She looks much like H. H. *when ill* & was very cordial & friendly. Goodnight darling I am very sleepy & do good to write you this much. Thine am I

I got here at 2 & leave at 9. E.D. dreamed all night of *you* (not me) & next day got my letter proposing to come here!! She only knew of you through a mention in my notice of Charlotte Hawes.

"Women talk: men are silent: that is why I dread women.

"My father only reads on Sunday—he reads *lonely* & *rigorous* books."

"If I read a book [and] it makes my whole body so cold no fire ever can warm me I know *that* is poetry. If I feel physically as if the top of my head were taken off, I know *that* is poetry. These are the only way I know it. Is there any other way."

"How do most people live without any thoughts. There are many people in the world (you must have noticed them in the street) How do they live. How do they get strength to put on their clothes in the morning"

"When I lost the use of my Eyes it was a comfort to think there were so few real *books* that I could easily find some one to read me all of them"

"Truth is such a *rare* thing it is delightful to tell it."

"I find ecstasy in living—the mere sense of living is joy enough"

I asked if she never felt want of employment, never going off the place & never seeing any visitor "I never thought of conceiving that I could ever have the slightest approach to such a want in all future time" (& added) "I feel that I have not expressed myself strongly enough."

She makes all the bread for her father only likes hers & says "& people must have pudding" this *very* dreamily, as if they were comets—so she makes them.

[That evening Higginson made this entry in his diary (HCL):]

To Amherst, arrived there at 2 Saw Prest Stearns, Mrs. Banfield & Miss Dickinson (twice) a remarkable experience, quite equalling my expectation. A pleasant country town, unspeakably quiet in the summer aftn.

[Next day he wrote his wife again, enclosing further notes (BPL), on ED. He dated the letter: Wednesday noon]:

342b

I am stopping for dinner at White River Junction, dearest, & in a few hours shall be at Littleton thence to go to Bethlehem. This morning at 9 I left Amherst & sent a letter last night. I shall mail this at L. putting with it another sheet about E.D. that is in my valise.

She said to me at parting "Gratitude is the only secret that cannot reveal itself."

I talked with Prest Stearns of Amherst about her—& found him a very pleasant companion in the cars. Before leaving today, I got in to the Museums & enjoyed them much; saw a meteoric stone almost as long as my arm & weighing 436 lbs! a big slice of some other planet. It fell in Colorado. The collection of bird tracks of extinct birds in stone is very wonderful & unique & other good things. I saw Mr. Dickinson this morning a little—thin dry & speechless—I saw what her life has been. Dr. S. says her sister is proud of her.

I wd. have stolen a *totty* meteor, dear but they were under glass.

Mrs. Bullard I have just met in this train with spouse & son—I shall ride up with her.

Some pretty glimpses of mts. but all is dry and burnt I never saw the river at Brattleboro so low.

Did I say I staid at Sargents in Boston & she still hopes for Newport.

This picture of Mrs Browning's tomb is from E.D. "Timothy Titcomb" [Dr. Holland] gave it to her.

I think I will mail this here as I hv. found time to write so much. I miss you little woman & wish you were here but you'd hate travelling.

Ever

E D again

"Could you tell me what home is"

"I never had a mother. I suppose a mother is one to whom you hurry when you are troubled."

"I never knew how to tell time by the clock till I was 15. My father thought he had taught me but I did not understand & I was afraid to say I did not & afraid to ask any one else lest he should know."

Her father was not severe I should think but remote. He did not wish them to read anything but the Bible. One day her brother brought home Kavanagh hid it under the piano cover & made signs to her & they read it: her father at last found it & was displeased. Perhaps it was before this that a student of his was amazed that they had never heard of Mrs. [Lydia Maria] Child & used to bring them books & hide in a bush by the door. They were then little things in short dresses with their feet on the rungs of the chair. After the first book she thought in ecstasy "This then is a book! And there are more of them!"

"Is it oblivion or absorption when things pass from our minds?"

Major Hunt interested her more than any man she ever saw. She remembered two things he said—that her great dog "understood gravitation" & when he said he should come again "in a year. If I say a shorter time it will be longer."

When I said I would come again *some time* she said "Say in a long time, that will be nearer. Some time is nothing."

After long disuse of her eyes she read Shakespeare & thought why is any other book needed.

I never was with anyone who drained my nerve power so much. Without touching her, she drew from me. I am glad not to live near her. She often thought me *tired* & seemed very thoughtful of others.

[The postscript of a letter Higginson wrote his sisters (HCL) on Sunday, 21 August, adds:]

Of course I hv. enjoyed my trip very very much. In Amherst I had a nice aftn & evng with my singular poetic correspondent & the remarkable cabinets of the College.

[Recalling the interview twenty years later, Higginson wrote in the *Atlantic Monthly* LXVIII (October 1891) 453:]

The impression undoubtedly made on me was that of an excess of tension, and of an abnormal life. Perhaps in time I could have got beyond that somewhat overstrained relation which not my will, but her needs, had forced upon us. Certainly I should have been most glad to bring it down to the level of simple truth and every-day comradeship; but it was not altogether easy. She was much too enigmatical a being for me to solve in an hour's interview, and an instinct told me that the slightest attempt at direct cross-examination would make her withdraw into her shell; I could only sit still and watch, as one does in the woods; I must name my bird without a gun, as recommended by Emerson.

E. MILLER BUDICK

The Dangers of the Living Word
(1985)

One of the most distinctive features of Emily Dickinson's poetic language is its wild animation and vital energy. Whether we choose to linger over each line or to read the poems at a clip, we cannot help but feel that in Dickinson's poetic worlds the very units of discourse—not the objects and events signified by words, but the words themselves—leap out at the reader like autonomous and freewheeling figures in a bold and vivid dance. In the following poem, for example, the metaphors and images of Dickinson's verse, capitalized and set off by dashes to declare their individuality and self-sufficiency, are in their own right the actors and sets that fill the stage of an intensely immediate drama.

> Blazing in Gold—and
> Quenching—in Purple!
> Leaping—like Leopards—in the sky—
> Then—at the feet of the old Horizon—
> Laying it's spotted face—to die!
>
> Stooping as low as the kitchen window—
> Touching the Roof—
> And tinting the Barn—
> Kissing it's Bonnet to the Meadow—
> And the Juggler of Day—is gone! (No. 228)[1]

The cast of verbal characters is so wide-ranging, so diversified, that it includes not only substantive nouns and names of objects, like "Leopards," but abstractions, adjectives, participles, and verbs—"Blazing" and "Quenching," for example, or, in other poems, "Knowing" and "Fearing" (No. 1218), "Accustomed" (No. 149), "Fitting" (No. 1277), "Going Home" (No. 1376), and "Ascertain" (No. 157), which by virtue of the way they are exaggerated and segregated in the text become independent members of Dickinson's dramatic companies. In fact, so basic and self-sufficient is each individual word for Dickinson that she can compound graceful, seemingly artless catalogues of terms such as birds, hours, bumblebee, grief, hills, and eternity, which ought to seem, by any of the ordinary rules of logic or grammar, nonparallel and shockingly dissimilar in quality or quantity or kind. In Dickinson's poem, however, they become congenial members of the poem's tantalizing cast.

> Some things that fly there be—
> Birds—Hours—the Bumblebee—
> Of these no Elegy.
>
> Some things that stay there be—
> Grief—Hills—Eternity—
> Nor this behooveth me.
>
> There are that resting, rise.
> Can I expound the skies?
> How still the Riddle lies! (No. 89)[2]

Many critics have commented on this special aliveness of the Dickinsonian word, on the verbal or "spectral" power of her verse, the "curious energy in the words and a tone like no other most of us have ever heard." Dickinson, to quote one critic, seems to have "perceived abstractions and thought sensations."

> A word is dead
> When it is said,
> Some say.
> I say it just
> Begins to live
> That day. (No. 1212)

It is not surprising, therefore, that her first concern when she writes to Colonel Thomas Wentworth Higginson in 1862 is whether or not her "Verse" is "alive," or that she worries in her second letter whether by dressing her thoughts in words those thoughts do not become stilted and "numb"

(LL 260 and 261). What critics have usually assumed or concluded about this Dickinsonian "passion for words" is that it expresses a "profound linguistic faith," a belief in the "saving power" of the word, and an unwavering confidence that language can "control nature and persons" and "say the unsayable."[3]

But if we pay careful attention to the specific kind of "power" that Dickinson's poetry displays, a troubling fact presents itself. "Blazing in Gold," for example, is certainly one of the poet's most enthusiastic cataloguings of the glorious events of nature. It offers, joyfully and exuberantly, a composite portrait of an exciting cosmic phenomenon. And yet it is a poem that trembles with a disturbing uncertainty. It quivers with hesitancy and doubt. Even before we begin to pore over the words and images for their deepest meanings, we sense that a vague but obstinate hint of uneasiness violates the poem's heady enthusiasm. The images seem frantic, almost embattled. There is, we may feel, more disruption in this poem than harmony. The very liveness of the language seems to threaten the cohesiveness of the poetic structure.

For all its ecstasy the poem harbors a subtle but definite intimation of unresolved human tension, a tension both emotional and sensual. For all the poem's integrity and wholeness, it implies disruption and disorder. This underlying chaos, which becomes more and more apparent as we begin to examine the poem carefully, first confronts us in the poetic texture. It is expressed obliquely but unmistakably in the poem's cracked and creviced surface, the words oddly capitalized and separated by eccentric dashes, the rhymes and rhythms slant and askew. Many critics have for one reason or another dismissed the irregularities of Dickinson's verse style, or, if not dismissed them, at least seriously underrated their function.[4] But the crazy-quilt surface of a poem like "Blazing in Gold" invites us to observe the universe from a new perspective. Subtly it coaxes us into recognizing how terribly frenzied, how frighteningly chaotic the otherwise serene, ebullient universe can seem.

The juggling act of day, for example, which represents both the natural appearance of day on the landscape and its poetic recreation in the poem, is not, Dickinson is warning, an unambiguous carnival of vibrant sensations. It can also be seen as a clownish pantomime of universe and language in apparent disarray. Day blazes, quenches, leaps, and dies—all perhaps, to no real purpose. It stoops, kisses, and then simply is "gone" in a veritable parody of meaningful action.

The details of the juggling act, therefore, which momentarily dazzle, can also terrify. The "Blazing in Gold," for example, and the "Quenching—in Purple," which have been thrown aloft by the adroit but dispassionate hand of the master juggler, are not just sensual events. They are principles of the natural order, two of the many balanced antitheses that are juggled simultaneously into momentary and unresolved suspension. Furthermore, not only do the opposed "Blazing" and "Quenching" represent a daily enactment of mutual annihilation, but each element incorporates its own principle of self-destruction. The blazing will eventually consume itself, if the quenching does not somehow succeed first; and the quenching is, by definition, not an additive substance but the absence of a substance, a power of cessation or deletion.

The poem's language reproduces a reality that flares and fizzles, excites and terrifies, at one and the same moment, a reality in which beauty and chaos, creation and destruction, exist side by side and in and through each other. Thus, the "Blazing" and "Quenching" that eventually cancel each other are balanced against each other on opposing lines; each self-annihilating force is isolated in its own stumbling fragment of speech. "Blazing in Gold—," the poem abruptly begins. The words are discrete and self-contained, set off not only from the "Quenching—in Purple" that is its direct negation, but also from the "and" that would connect it to any other natural event. "And," the poem continues, "Quenching—in Purple." The phrase is not only detached from the "Blazing" that is its opposite but is internally splintered between the "Quenching" that does not have sensuous existence and the "Purple" that does. Words that live can die; worse, they can even kill.

What the poem is trying to do, then, is not simply to describe day and sunset in the most graphic terms available, but to sketch out, as a working hypothesis, something not unlike the idealist configuration of reality in which dissolution follows emanation and a host of glittering phenomena occupy the ground between. (I will have more to say about the relevance of idealism later.) The poem, in this view, is not about harmonious interrelation, nor is it about unity and its reattainment since, from the vantage point of this state of the cosmos, unity exists only after phenomenal reality has disappeared to a realm beyond the powers of human knowledge and human language. But the poem is about the explosion into phenomenal being that defines the world as we know it. The poem's central strategy is to delineate a oneness that is really a seething competition of irreconcilable opposites, a "Blazing" and a "Quenching," that defy one another, or, to use another of the poem's special metaphors, a spotted leopard whose leap to the sky is both magnificent and menacing and who threatens cosmic serenity only to find himself the victim of his own threat and his own mortality. Reality, Dickinson implies, may be a juggling act that is indistinguishable from the juggler. It may be a hydra-like creature whose integrity is compounded of inharmonious, disjointed, and unrelated facets and phenomena and that is juggled into fragmentary existence by its own propensity to juggle.

This is not to deny the exquisite beauty portrayed in the poem. For Dickinson, however, beauty may be yoked to the very elements of cosmic disunity that seem to defy it. It may be fashioned of the components that seem to our partial, mortal vision to attempt its destruction. Beauty, therefore, may affect us not serenely, but turbulently. It may arouse in us fears more powerful than the sense of ecstasy for which we would like to believe nature has been created. Thus a pattern of cosmic disruption and accompanying human tension vibrates beneath the surface of "Blazing in Gold." Disruption and tension seem, paradoxically, both to contradict cosmic beauty and perfection and to represent their key constituents.

NOTES

¹ I have reproduced the variorum copy of this poem, located in packet 23 (H 127 a) of Dickinson's works. The manuscript copy in the Houghton Library is even more erratically punctuated and capitalized than Johnson's typescript suggests.

² For an interesting discussion of this poem, see David T. Porter. *The Art of Emily Dickinson's Early Poetry* (Cambridge, Mass., 1966), 32.

³ On Dickinson's "spectral" power and the power to "say the unsayable," see Louise Bogan, "A Mystical Poet," in Archibald MacLeish, Louise Bogan, and Richard Wilbur (eds.), *Emily Dickinson, Three Views: Papers Delivered at Amherst College . . . October 23, 1959* (Amherst, Mass., 1960), 34; on her "curious energy," see Archibald MacLeish, "The Private World," in MacLeish, Bogan, and Wilbur (eds.), *Three Views,* 16–19; and on her "linguistic faith" and "saving power," see Elinor Wilner, "The Poetics of Emily Dickinson," *ELH,* XXXVIII (1971), 126–54; see also George Frisbie Whicher, *This Was a Poet: A Critical Biography of Emily Dickinson* (Ann Arbor, 1957), 227–49; Inder Nath Kher, *The Landscape of Absence: Emily Dickinson's Poetry* (New Haven, 1974), 32; Brita Lindberg-Seyersted, *The Voice of the Poet: Aspects of Style in the Poetry of Emily Dickinson* (Cambridge, Mass., 1968); David Porter, "Emily Dickinson: The Poetics of Doubt," *ESQ: A Journal of the American Renaissance,* LX (1970), 86–88; Rebecca Patterson, "The Cardinal Points Symbolism of Emily Dickinson (I)," *Midwest Quarterly,* XIV (1973), 206; Donald E. Thackrey, *Emily Dickinson's Approach to Poetry, University of Nebraska Studies* (Lincoln, 1954), 62; and Charles R. Anderson, *Emily Dickinson's Poetry: Stairway of Surprise* (New York, 1960), 30–46, 91ff., and 300–307. Even Col. Higginson comments on the "strange power" of Dickinson's poetry (L 330 a). Very recently Sharon Cameron, *Lyric Time: Dickinson and the Limits of Genre* (Baltimore, 1979), and David Porter, *Dickinson: The Modern Idiom* (Cambridge, Mass., 1981), have brought the matter of Dickinson's eccentric use of language into a contemporary context. See also Geoffrey H. Hartman's discussion of language in "Words and Wounds," in *Saving the Text: Literature / Derrida / Philosophy* (Baltimore, 1981), 118–57.

⁴ For a different reading of this poem see Anderson, *Stairway of Surprise*, 135–38; cf. 122. For representative approaches to the typographic appearance of Dickinson's poems see Thomas H. Johnson, "Introduction," in *The Poems of Emily Dickinson*, 3 vols. (Cambridge, Mass., 1976), lxiii; R. W. Franklin, *The Editing of Emily Dickinson: A Reconsideration* (Madison, 1967), 120–21; Brita Lindberg-Seyersted, "Emily Dickinson's Punctuation," *Studia Neophilologica*, XXXVII (1965), 349–50; Wilner, "The Poetics of Emily Dickinson," 126 and 138; Roland Hagenbüchle, "Precision and Indeterminacy in the Poetry of Emily Dickinson," *ESQ: A Journal of the American Renaissance*, XX (1974), 54; and Robert Weisbuch, *Emily Dickinson's Poetry* (Chicago, 1972), 73. See also Porter, *Emily Dickinson's Early Poetry*, 140–45; Anderson, *Stairway of Surprise*, 300–307; John Crowe Ransom, "Emily Dickinson: A Poet Restored," in Richard B. Sewall (ed.), *Emily Dickinson: A Collection of Critical Essays* (Englewood Cliffs, N.J., 1963), 88–89; and Edith Stamm, "Poetry and Punctuation," *Saturday Review*, XLVI (March 30, 1963), 20–29.

JUDITH FARR

Art as Life
(1992)

> When Time's course closed, and Death was encountered at the end, barring with fleshless arm the portals of Eternity, how Genius still held close his dying bride, sustained her through the agony of the passage, bore her triumphant into his own home—heaven; restored her, redeemed, to Jehovah— her maker; and at last, before Angel and Archangel, crowned her with the crown of Immortality.
>
> —Charlotte Brontë, *Shirley* (1849)

In April 1884 a statue of John Harvard by Daniel Chester French (1850–1931) was unveiled in Harvard Yard. French was the son of a prominent New England lawyer; as a boy he lived in Amherst. His family were friends of Susan Dickinson, and he himself was a favorite of Emily Dickinson's Norcross cousins. French's statue of *The Minute Man* (1874), commissioned by fellow townsfolk of Concord, made him famous. He would go on to sculpt some of the best-known statues in the United States—not only *John Harvard* but the seated portrait for the *Lincoln* memorial (dedicated in 1922). Sue and the Norcrosses must have kept Emily acquainted with developments in the career of the fifteen-year-old Danny French she once knew. The Dickinsons had affectionate ties with Harvard.[1] When the statue was unveiled, Dickinson was apparently moved by French's success in so distinguished a sphere. She wrote to him,

> Dear Mr. French:—
>   We learn with delight of the recent acquisition to your fame, and hasten to congratulate you on an honor so reverently won.
>   Success is dust, but an aim forever touched with dew.
>   God keep you fundamental!
>
>> Circumference, thou bride
>> Of awe,—possessing, thou
>> Shalt be possessed by
>> Every hallowed knight
>> That dares to covet thee.
>
>   Yours faithfully,
>   Emily Dickinson (L 3.822)

Her letter was preserved by French's family and, indeed, it is among the most significant and touching of the letters, especially if one considers her circumstances when it was written. In 1884 she was just two years from death and, for the most part, unknown as a poet. French was only thirty-four, with one triumph behind him and many others ahead. There can be no more public art, perhaps, than commemorative sculpture; unlike some other public art forms—music or theater—it aspires to material continuity and permanence. French's statues would stand in the open, buffeted by winds and snow. They were images whose very purpose was publicity: to proclaim the enduring greatness of a public man. By their nature, then, French's calling and work were distant from the remarkably private life and art of the woman who addressed him. Yet Dickinson's letter salutes French as (he may not have known) a fellow artist. From her triple isolation as a recluse, an elderly and dependent spinster, and a poet whose eccentricities were better known than her verses, she offered him a few words of advice.

Thus: honor was to be "reverently won." She assumes that he has done so, but her earnest phrase reminds him of it. The honor of being chosen to do the statue is conflated with the honor that belongs to artists when they are faithful to the sacred mission of telling all the truth in the "slant" way that is Art itself. To win such honor in poetry, if only in her own mind, Dickinson had worked very hard. She realized that an artist must be satisfied with the artifact; otherwise, its recognition by others is hollow, even nugatory. She had written, about twenty years earlier,

Fame of Myself, to justify,
All other Plaudit be
Superfluous—An Incense
Beyond Necessity—

Fame of Myself to lack—Although
My Name be else Supreme—
This were an Honor honorless—
A futile Diadem—(713)

Such austere advice might appropriately be given to sculptors, who are es-
pecially vulnerable to the public taste by a need for commissions; but it im-
plies Dickinson's proud, self-reliant avoidance of any praise that might be
earned by a violation of aesthetic vision. And it reminds us once again of the
limitations of those who surrounded her when it came to reading her poetry.
Of people with literary connections—the essayist Higginson, the editors
Samuel Bowles and Josiah Holland, the novelist Helen Hunt Jackson and
her sister-in-law Sue—only the two women intuited Dickinson's greatness.
Jackson begged Dickinson repeatedly to accept her help in publishing. "You
are a great poet," she wrote, accusing her of being stingy in keeping back her
poems:

> What portfolios of verses you must have.—
> It is a cruel wrong to your "day & generation" that you will not give them
> light.—if such a thing should happen as that I should outlive you, I wish you
> would make me your literary legatee & executor. Surely, after you are what is
> called "dead," you will be willing that the poor ghosts you have left behind,
> should be cheered and pleased by your verses, will you not?—You ought to
> be.—I do not think we have a right to withhold from the world a word or a
> thought any more than a *deed,* which might help a single soul.[2]

This enthusiasm resulted in the anonymous appearance of "Success
is counted sweetest" in *Masque of Poets.* Other poems of the 1860s were
"stolen" by Sue or Bowles for the *Springfield Republican.* Just after she mar-
ried, Sue compared inaugurating Emily's career to launching the ship *Burn-
side:* she was its promoter but it was taking too much time.[3] Jackson's clever
appeal to Dickinson's thoughtfulness for others was matched in later years
by requests that she lend poems to charitable publications. From such en-
treaties Dickinson always fled, securing the intervention and assistance of
Colonel Higginson. She asked him on one occasion, "May I tell [Mrs. Jack-
son] . . . that you dont prefer it?" It seemed to her "sordid" to refuse requests

for poems on her own account. (L 2.566). But refuse she must, and did. She seems to have perceived that any interest shown in her poetry by Higginson and Bowles originated, finally, in personal affection. By the mid-1860s Sue's admiration did not include encouragements to publish. And there is evidence that Dickinson recognized the difference between her poetic language and the popular verse of her day:

> Honor is then the safest hue
> In a posthumous Sun—
> Not any color will endure
> That scrutiny can burn (1671)

In her copy of Emerson's *Poems,* she put an X next to "Woodnotes," with its lines

> For this present, hard
> Is the fortune of the bard,
>   Born out of time;
> All his accomplishment,
> From Nature's utmost treasure spent,
>   Booteth not him.

Thus there was a persuasive logic in Dickinson's various allusions to the inner security a poet requires: "Himself—to Him—a Fortune—/ Exterior—to Time" (448). Her words to French, "We learn with delight of . . . your fame," came from the same hand that had written, so realistically, a few years earlier,

> Fame is the one that does not stay—
> It's occupant must die
> Or out of sight of estimate
> Ascend incessantly—
> Or be that most insolvent thing
> A Lightning in the Germ—
> Electrical the embryo
> But we demand the Flame (1475)

In this poem she grouped herself, as usual, with the "we" who are not famous or, as in "This was a Poet" (448), not artists. Yet I think she may have hoped that she was the lightning in the germ of another age; hence she left no instructions to her sister Lavinia to destroy the locked box containing seven hundred poems. The famous letter she sent to Higginson when he told her to "delay 'to publish'" is tinged with romantic grandiosity, as well as Puritan reserve, but it seems wholly sincere:

> If fame belonged to me, I could not escape her—if she did not, the longest day would pass me on the chase—and the approbation of my Dog, would forsake me—then—My Barefoot-Rank is better (L 2.408)

She had great belief in herself, if we take her first sentence seriously. Yet she must also have known her art to be "insolvent" in such a marketplace as the Boston or New York of her lifetime. There Bowles's associate Holland, who also recommended that Dickinson not publish, had been able to sell to *Scribner's* the following lines for his dog. Dickinson read them aloud in 1881 to her delighted mother and Vinnie "at their request" (L 3.706):

> Did I sit fondly at His feet,
> As you, dear Blanco, sit at mine,
> And watch Him with a love as sweet,
> My life would grow divine!

Her only acknowledgment of the verse's bathos was a witty remark to Elizabeth Holland, "Doctor's betrothal to 'Blanco' I trust you bear unmurmuringly" (L 3.706).

"Success is dust," she tells French, "but an aim forever touched with dew." This line, like the remaining sentences in her letter, contains words she endowed with special meaning. Perhaps her most anthologized poem would be the clear-sighted and bittersweet "Success is counted sweetest / By those who ne'er succeed" (67). When *Poems* (1890) appeared, it was placed on the first page. It drew its imagery from two wars: the Civil War and that war—also "civil" or between two compulsions or forces—fought by those "Who charge within the bosom / The Cavalry of Woe" (126). "Success is counted sweetest" was probably written when Dickinson was only twenty-nine. Its sad wisdom embraces her remark to French a quarter of a century later. Success is dust because it is as capricious as fame; it is associated with death, since only the ruined and dying really understand or (vicariously) experience it:

> Not one of all the purple Host
> Who took the Flag today
> Can tell the definition
> So clear of Victory

As he defeated—dying—
On whose forbidden ear
The distant strains of triumph
Burst agonized and clear!

Nevertheless, success is "an aim forever touched with dew," and *dew* is a word that Dickinson had long associated with creativity. Artists want to be successful; it is only natural. "Dew" belongs to fresh mornings full of new chances; it is akin to inspiration; it is nature's baptismal grace. Dickinson's letter cautions French that success may fade and is valuable only as an aim, an incitement to creation. Still (living in the America of Horace Greeley) she recognizes it to be a lure "forever."

If French had read her poems, as is unlikely, Dickinson's prayer "God keep you fundamental" might have seemed to him especially persuasive. *Fundamental* is one of her touchstones for poetry; she uses it revealingly in five poems (997, 1106, 1205, 1295, 1744). To be fundamental means to be essential, to remember the foundations of things, to look into their component parts and disclose the harmony of the whole. Her choice of the word in this specific instance, in speaking to a sculptor, is wonderfully apt. She tells French to remember the basic materials with which he works. Marble, brass, or stone, they are all describable in the end as "earth." She hopes he will be an honest artist, true to the humble elements he must employ, and true to life.

Her deeply felt exclamation leads to a verse that includes several other critical Dickinson terms: circumference, bride, awe, knight. From her isolation she addresses the famous youth in words that show her own long intimacy with the muse:

Circumference, thou bride
Of awe,—possessing, thou
Shalt be possessed by
Every hallowed knight
That dares to covet thee.

I have said that it is characteristic of Dickinson to trace artistic inspiration to love. Even more, she associates it with marriage. Her word "circumference" generally means either poetry itself or the significance of all that exists, on earth and in heaven. She marries it here to awe: the respectful fear or veneration that should be chief dweller in God's universe. The poetry or circumference of things possesses every knight—art, like chivalry, is a noble venture—who dares to know it, in the biblical (sexual) sense of coveting. Yet this coveting and possession of the bride Circumference are not wrong, for the knight is hallowed, honorable. Her words, then, tell French that he must be honorably married to the muse, to "poetry" or beauty and truth. She signs her letter with the rare "Faithfully," a word that implies commitment, not only to her friend French but to the ideals expressed in her letter.

In her last years, speaking of aesthetics, she talked with authority. Love was increasingly her subject, love as the essential element in all understanding. To her nephew Ned, on vacation in the Adirondacks, she wrote, "Your intimacy with the Mountains I heartily endorse—Ties more Eleusinian I must leave to you—Deity will guide you—I do not mean Jehovah—The little God with Epaulettes" (L 3.880). Eros with his bow and arrows would come to Ned's aid; she hoped he would marry. But nature, art, and love were commingled for her; whether advising nephews or sculptors, she insisted on the connection. Much of her advice was given to young men. Samuel Bowles Jr. was marrying in 1883. She congratulated him with words echoing Revelation 21:21 that included her old symbol for bliss associated with his father, Eden: "Every several Gate is of one Pearl" (L 3.796). A poem she sent him resembles her lines for French. Written within a few months of one another, each lyric declares the importance of love to life and art. Her poem for Bowles's son—a writer and journalist and therefore an aspirant to the artistic life—enjoins,

> Lad of Athens, faithful be
> To Thyself,
> And Mystery—
> All the rest is Perjury (L 3.797)

As she did with French, Dickinson exhorts Bowles to be true to his own vision and yet to the mystery of creation. Athens was the great seat of classical civilization, the home of everyone who loved learning. The subtext of her poem is another, however, which was written by Lord Byron in 1810:

> Maid of Athens, ere we part,
> Give, oh give me back my heart!
> Or, since that has left my breast,
> Keep it now, and take the rest!

Byron's pledge to his Greek maid is "My life, I love you." By appealing to it in her poem for young Bowles, Dickinson is alluding once again to the metaphor of passionate vows that orders her poem for French. To all her

"Kingdom of [young] Knights" (L 3.876), with their futures before them, the aging Emily Dickinson wrote that love and honor are requisite to artistic endeavor.

NOTES

1   Sewall reports Edward Dickinson's "lifelong loyalty" to Yale College, where he graduated in the class of 1823 (*Life,* p. 45). His son Austin, however, was sent to Amherst College, graduating in the class of 1850. He then went to Harvard Law School, graduating in July 1854. This connection seems to have displaced the Yale tie, and the Dickinson papers in the immediate family's possession went to Harvard.

2   Leyda, II, 431. Leyda, Jay. *The Years & Hours of Emily Dickinson* (New Haven: Yale, 1960).

3   Sue sent a message to ED after the publication in the *Republican* of "Safe in their Alabaster Chambers" on March 1, 1862: "*Has girl read Republican?* It takes as long to start our Fleet as the Burnside." Leyda, II, 48.

SANDRA M. GILBERT

The Wayward Nun beneath the Hill: Emily Dickinson and the Mysteries of Womanhood
(1983)

Young Mabel Loomis Todd had been living for two months in Amherst, Massachusetts, where her husband, David, had just been appointed Director of the Amherst College Observatory, when on November 6, 1881, she wrote her parents an enthusiastic letter about one of the town's most fascinating citizens:

> I must tell you about the *character* of Amherst. It is a lady whom the people call the *Myth.* She is a sister of Mr. Dickinson, & seems to be the climax of all the family oddity. She has not been outside of her own house in fifteen years, except once to see a new church, when she crept out at night, & viewed it by moonlight. No one who calls upon her mother & sister ever see her, but she allows little children once in a great while, & one at a time, to come in, when she gives them cake or candy, or some nicety, for she is very fond of little ones. But more often she lets down the sweetmeat by a string, out of

a window, to them. She dresses wholly in white, & her mind is said to be perfectly wonderful. She writes finely, but no one *ever* sees her. Her sister, who was at Mrs. Dickinson's party, invited me to come & sing to her mother sometime. . . . People tell me the *myth* will hear every note—she will be near, but unseen. . . . Isn't that like a book? So interesting.[1]

By now that letter has become almost as famous as the Mythic Miss Dickinson herself, largely because it seems to have contributed to a process of mystification and fictionalization that surrounded one of America's greatest writers with what Thomas Wentworth Higginson once called a "fiery mist."[2]

Higginson himself also, of course, contributed to this process that transformed a reclusive poet-cook into a New England Nun of Love-and-Art.[3] More than a decade before Mabel Todd recorded the rumours she had heard about "the rare mysterious Emily,"[4] he visited his self-styled "Scholar" in her Amherst home, and though his notes on the meeting are not as gothic as the stories Mrs. Todd reported to her parents, they add both fire and mist to the mythic portrait, with their description of how there was "a step like a pattering child's in entry" and "a little plain woman . . . in a very plain & exquisitely clean white pique . . . came to me with two day lilies, which she put in a sort of childlike way into my hand & said, 'These are my introduction' in a soft frightened breathless childlike voice. . . ."[5] Interestingly enough, moreover, even the "little plain woman's" most prosaic remarks seemed to enhance the evolving Myth with just the dash of paradox needed to give a glimmer of irony to the dramatic halo around her: "She makes all the bread," Higginson observed, "for her father only likes hers & says, '& people must have puddings,' this *very* dreamily, as if they were comets—so she makes them."[6]

After her death, in fact, a number of Dickinson's admirers like to dwell on that ineffable glimmer of irony. "Even though her mind might be occupied with 'all mysteries and all knowledge,' including meteors and comets, her hands were often busy in most humble household ways," wrote her cousin Helen Knight Wyman in a 1905 article for the *Boston Cooking School Magazine* on "Emily Dickinson as Cook and Poetess."[7] She "wrote indefatigably as some women cook or knit," added R. P. Blackmur in 1937.[8] As the Myth grew and glowed, drama, domesticity, and Dickinson seem to have become inseparable. It is no wonder, then—given this unlikely, often absurdly literary image of an obsessively childlike, gothic yet domestic spinster—that recent readers of Dickinson's verse have struggled to deconstruct the "Myth of Amherst" and discover instead the aesthetic technician, the intellectual, and the visionary, whose lineaments would seem to have been blurred or obliterated in the "fiery mist" generated not by the poet herself but by her friends and admirers.

I want to argue here, however, that though their fictionalizations may sometimes have been crude or melodramatic, Mabel Loomis Todd, Thomas Wentworth Higginson, and many others were not in fact projecting their own fantasies onto the comparatively neutral (if enigmatic) figure of Emily Dickinson. Rather, as I will suggest, all these observers were responding to a process of self-mythologizing that led Dickinson herself to use all the materials of daily reality, and most especially the details of domesticity, as if they were not facts but metaphors, in order to recreate herself-and-her-life as a single, emblematic text, and often, indeed, as a sort of religious text— the ironic hagiography, say, of a New England Nun. More specifically, I want to suggest that Dickinson structured this life/text around a series of "mysteries" that were distinctively female, deliberately exploring and exploiting the characteristics, even the constraints, of nineteenth-century womanhood so as to transform and transcend them.

Finally, I want to argue that such a provisional and analytic acceptance of the Dickinson Myth may serve the reality of Dickinson's art better than the contemptuous rejection of legend that has lately become fashionable. For by deciphering rather than deconstructing the intricate text of this poet's life, we may come closer to understanding the methods and materials of her actual, literary texts. Throughout this essay, therefore, I will try to "read" biographical mysteries, and I will use the word "mystery" in almost all the current as well as a few of the archaic senses given by the OED. These include "a religious truth known only from divine revelation"; "a mystical presence"; a "religious . . . rite, especially a sacramental rite of the Christian religion"; "an incident in the life of [Christ] regarded . . . as having a mystical significance"; "a hidden or secret thing . . . a riddle or enigma"; "a 'secret' or highly technical operation in a trade or art"; a secret rite; a "miracle-play"; "a service, occupation; office, ministry"; "a handicraft, craft, art, trade, profession, or calling"; and finally "a kind of plum cake." All these senses of "mystery"—even, or perhaps especially, the plum cake—have some application to both the Myth and the mythmaking of Emily Dickinson.

For like her Romantic precursor John Keats, one of the poets to whom she turned most often for sustenance, Dickinson understood that a "life of any worth is a continual allegory." [9] Thus she ambitiously undertook to live (and to create) "a life like the scriptures, figurative—which [some] people can no more make out than they can the hebrew Bible." Such a life, as Keats observed, need not be theatrical; one might be both public and melodramatic without achieving true significance. "Lord Byron cuts a figure—but he is not figurative—," Keats commented wryly, and Dickinson would have seen such a remark as offering her permission to dramatize the private "trivia" of domesticity, rather than public turmoil, permission even to conflate puddings and comets. For again, like Keats, she would have perceived the essential reciprocity of the life/text and the literary text. About Shakespeare, for instance, Keats famously observed that he "led a life of Allegory: his works are the comments on it."[10] But as I hope to show, the same striking statement can be made about the mysteries Dickinson enacted and allegorized.

Dickinson's impulse to enact mysteries can be traced back almost to her childhood. Two episodes from her year at Mount Holyoke, for instance, seem to have signalled what was on the way. The first is one that Mabel Todd claimed to have heard about from the poet's sister Vinnie. The seventeen-year-old Emily, wrote Mrs. Todd, "was never floored. When the Euclid examination came and she had never studied it, she went to the blackboard and gave such a glib exposition of imaginary figures that the dazed teacher passed her with the highest mark."[11] The second episode is more famous and has been widely discussed, even by biographers and critics who dislike the "Myth of Amherst." Throughout Dickinson's time at Mount Holyoke, the school was in the throes of an evangelical revival eagerly encouraged by Mary Lyon, the school's founder and principal. According to Clara Newman Turner, there was an occasion when "Miss Lyon . . . asked all those who wanted to be Christians to rise. The wording of the request was not such as Emily could honestly accede to and she remained seated—the only one who did not rise."[12]

In these two episodes, we can discern the seeds of personal and religious mysteries that Dickinson was to develop and dramatize throughout both her life/text and her literary texts. Moreover, these two episodes suggest that we can reduce the major Dickinsonian mysteries to two categories: mystery as puzzle (secret, riddle, enigma, or blackboard battle with imaginary figures), and mystery as miracle (mystic transformation, inexplicable sacrament, or private parallel to traditional Christian professions of faith). If we bear these two categories in mind as we meditate on Dickinson's "life as Allegory," we find that, on the one hand, at the center of this poet's self-mythologizing mystery-as-puzzle we confront a kind of absence or blank, the enigmatic wound that many biographers have treated as if it were the subject of a romantic detective novel called "The Mystery of the Missing Lover." At the center of the Dickinson mystery-as-miracle, on the other hand, we encounter a presence or power, the "white heat" (365) of Dickinson's art, whose

story we might label "The Mystery of the Muse." Yet these two mysteries—
we might also call them the mysteries of Life and Art—are of course con-
nected. For, even more than most other writers, Emily Dickinson the poet
mysteriously transformed the pain associated with the puzzle at the center
of her life into the miracle of her art; through that transformation, indeed,
she became the "Myth of Amherst."

NOTES

[1] Jay Leyda, *The Years and Hours of Emily Dickinson*, 2 vols. (New Haven: Yale University Press, 1960), vol. 2, p. 357.

[2] See T. W. Higginson to ED, in *The Letters of Emily Dickinson*, 3 vols., ed. Thomas H. Johnson (Cambridge: Harvard University Press, 1958), vol. 2, p. 461: "I have the greatest desire to see you, always feeling that perhaps if I could once take you by the hand I might be something to you; but till then you only enshroud yourself in this fiery mist & I cannot reach you, but only rejoice in the rare sparkles of light."

[3] For a newspaper story about a real "New England Nun" whose career would have been known to Dickinson, see Leyda, vol. 1, p. 148. For a fictionalized account of a "New England Nun" that mythologizes female domesticity in a way partly (though not wholly) comparable to Dickinson's own, see Mary E. Wilkins Freeman, "A New England Nun," in *A New England Nun and Other Stories* (New York: Harper & Row, 1891).

[4] Leyda, vol. 2, p. 376.

[5] Ibid., p. 151.

[6] Ibid.

[7] *The Boston Cooking-School Magazine*, June–July 1906.

[8] Quoted by James Reeves in an *Introduction to the Selected Poems of Emily Dickinson* reprinted in *Emily Dickinson: A Collection of Critical Essays*, ed. Richard B. Sewall (Englewood Cliffs, N.J.: Prentice-Hall, 1963), p. 119.

[9] John Keats, to George and Georgiana Keats, Friday, Feb. 18, 1819.

[10] Ibid.

[11] Leyda, vol. 1, p. 131.

[12] Ibid., p. 135.

RICHARD B. SEWALL

Early Friendships II
(1974)

If we would know more about the Amherst girls in Emily's circle, our ignorance about the young men is even more tantalizing. The problem, of course, is documentation. It has been estimated that we have about a tenth of all the letters Emily Dickinson wrote, and probably less than a thousandth of those written to her. The letter to Abiah, Emily Fowler, Jane Humphrey, and Susan Gilbert allow us to talk fairly confidently about these young ladies, although we would give a great deal to know what they wrote to her. But as for the young men who we know came almost daily in and out of the Dickinson house, spent many an evening in talk and currant wine, escorted the Dickinson girls to lectures, concerts, sleigh rides, promenades, and all the other functions a college town with its inexhaustible supply of young males can provide—as for these, the source of much of the color of Emily's young life, we have little more than bits and scraps, an invitation here and there, a few valentines, and brief, often cryptic, messages.

And where the allurements of romance coincide with a knowledge vacuum, legends flourish. They have flourished, unfortunately, here. Most of the rumors center on Edward Dickinson as chief spoiler of his daughter's chances of romantic happiness, and speculation has been active from the first as to who among the dozen or so frequenters of the Dickinson household broke Emily's heart and cut her life in two. The dubious assumption behind it all is that Emily was staking her life on romantic happiness and, when that failed her, gave up and withdrew. At this point we would do well to look at the leading contenders and assess what we actually do know about them. This process may, in turn, help resolve the problem.

One certainty is that Benjamin Franklin Newton, a law student in Edward Dickinson's office from 1847 to 1849, was important in Emily's formative years. She herself said so. The evidence is firm, although it comes not from any surviving correspondence between the two but mainly from a letter Emily wrote, shortly after Newton's death early in 1853, to his minister in Worcester, the Reverend Mr. Edward Everett Hale. Newton was nine years older than Emily, a young man of rare qualities and the first (with the possible exception of Leonard Humphrey) whom Emily regarded as one of those older men she called variously her tutor, preceptor, or master. Her letter to Hale, of whom she inquired as to Newton's spiritual state at the time of his death, is one of the few we have addressed to a complete stranger. It is formal, yet simple, direct, and almost entirely free from the sentimental pose of the elegiac passage on Humphrey. This time, she is more concerned with the deceased than with herself, and her account of Newton is objective and discerning. The style is under full control.

Rev Mr Hale—

Pardon the liberty Sir, which a stranger takes in addressing you, but I think you may be familiar with the last hours of a Friend, and I therefore transgress a courtesy, which in another circumstance, I should seek to observe. I think, Sir, you were the Pastor of Mr B. F. Newton, who died sometime since in Worcester, and I often have hoped to know if his last hours were cheerful, and if he was willing to die. Had I his wife's acquaintance, I w'd not trouble you Sir, but I have never met her, and do not know where she resides, nor have I a friend in Worcester who could satisfy my inquiries. You may think my desire strange, Sir, but the Dead was dear to me, and I would love to know that he sleeps peacefully.

Mr. Newton was with my Father two years, before going to Worcester— in pursuing his studies, and was much in our family.

I was then but a child, yet I was old enough to admire the strength, and grace, of an intellect far surpassing my own, and it taught me many lessons, for which I thank it humbly, now that it is gone. Mr Newton became to me a gentle, yet grave Preceptor, teaching me what to read, what authors to admire, what was most grand or beautiful in nature, and that sublimer lesson, a faith in things unseen, and in a life again, nobler, and much more blessed—

Of all these things he spoke—he taught me of them all, earnestly, tenderly, and when he went from us, it was as an elder brother, loved indeed very much, and mourned, and remembered. During his life in Worcester, he often wrote to me, and I replied to his letters—I always asked for his health, and he answered so cheerfully, that while I knew he was ill, his death indeed surprised me. He often talked of God, but I do not know certainly if he was his Father in Heaven—Please Sir, to tell me if he was willing to die, and if you think him at Home. I should love so much to know certainly, that he was today in Heaven. Once more, Sir, please forgive the audacities of a Stranger, and a few lines, Sir, from you, at a convenient hour, will be received with gratitude, most happy to requite you, sh'd it have opportunity.

Yours very respectfully,
Emily E. Dickinson

P.S. Please address your reply to Emily E. Dickinson—Amherst— Mass—

Why Emily should have worried about Mr. Hale's thinking it strange of her to ask if Newton were "willing to die" is itself strange, since the question was a common one in her day. It was a test of faith. Such a question need not mean that she was obsessed or overburdened with thoughts of death. Her inquiry was the first of many similar ones she directed to men, mostly ministerial and always older than she, whom she regarded as able to help her with ultimate questions—the sort of questions, according to the letter, Newton must have talked to her about when he was her "grave Preceptor."

The letter clearly defines Newton's role as older brother, criterion intellect, friend and guide in matters aesthetic and spiritual. We see Emily, in her mid-teens, already reaching out for the qualities of a mind "far surpassing" her own, and responding to its "gentle, yet grave" instruction. She loved him—he "was dear to me"—but whatever romantic hopes she may have had are not apparent in her restrained rhetoric. It was Newton who, the year after he left Edward Dickinson's office, sent her a copy of Emerson's poems,[1] and it is generally thought that he was the "friend [she wrote Higginson in 1862] who taught me Immortality—but venturing too near, himself—he never returned—"[2] Twice she spoke of him as her earliest friend. Three days after he died (March 24, 1853) she wrote a brief postscript to a long and cheerful letter to Austin (perhaps another instance of telling "no one the cause of my grief"):

> Love from us all. Monday noon. Oh Austin, Newton is dead. The first of my own friends. Pace.

The letter to Hale, for whatever reason, waited a full nine months. His reply, if any, has not survived. She wrote him again, "several springs" later (1856?):

> My dear Mr. Hale.
> Perhaps you forget a Stranger Maid, who several springs ago—asked of a friend's Eternity—, and if in her simplicity—, she still remembers you, and culls for you a Rose and hopes upon a purer morn, to pluck you buds serener— please pardon her, and them.
>
> > With sweet respect
> > Your friend,
> > Emily E. Dickinson

Twenty years later, Newton was still on her mind (to Higginson, spring 1876):

My earliest friend wrote me the week before he died "If I live, I will go to Amherst—if I die, I certainly will."

Newton's greatest distinction is that among all her early friends, male or female, he seems to be the only one who understood her poetic promise—or the only one, at least, for whom there is evidence that this is so. There are two scraps, slim but convincing. The first is an inscription he wrote in Emily's autograph album before he left Amherst:

All can write Autographs, but few paragraphs; for we are mostly no more than *names*.

The second is a remark of Emily's in her third letter to Higginson thanking him for his criticism of her poetry. The passage indicates not only Newton's influence in shaping her career but how early it was (at least 1853, when Newton died) she began thinking of herself as a poet.

My dying Tutor told me that he would like to live till I had been a poet, but Death was much of Mob as I could master—then—

Newton's discernment underscores, of course, the lack of it in her other friends and advisors like Higginson, Emily Fowler Ford, Dr. Holland, Samuel Bowles. His death, coming at a time when the distance between Emily and all her young friends was growing, cut off her most promising hope for literary guidance and encouragement. Looking back, she may have seen how serious his loss was, and our wonder lessens at her hyperbole when she told Higginson in 1862 that "for several years, my Lexicon—was my only companion—"

Nevertheless, to take this remark to Higginson literally and regard Emily as lonely and bereft for the several years following March 24, 1853, is to succumb to her hyperbole and slip into a stock aspect of the Myth. The annals of the town and her family record enough activity, social and otherwise, for the next year or so to make any such simplification of her life impossible. Her friendship with Sue was still warm; they were seeing a great deal of each other. She wrote to Sue in September 1854 about having "a great deal of company"—the suggestion is, too much. And there were at least two young men, her distant cousin John Graves and his friend Henry Vaughan Emmons, who paid her much—and welcome—attention until they graduated from the college (Emmons in 1854, Graves in 1855) and went their ways.

Perhaps John Graves, simply because of his cousinship (Emily habitually addressed him as "Cousin John"), should not count as a romantic possibility, although he was an exceptionally handsome and capable young man. Born in Sunderland, he was a year younger than Emily and related to the Dickinsons through the Gunn family. He made his first call on his kinsfolk early in his freshman year and was a frequent visitor from then on. Emily went to a concert with him, knitted wristlets for him, played music for him, asked him in (with Emmons) for currant wine. During the family's Washington visit in 1854, Emily and Susan Gilbert were left behind in the Pleasant Street house under Graves's protection. When he and Emmons quarreled during his junior year, Emily was much concerned for his happiness and rejoiced at their reconciliation.

Her letters to him, except two, are mostly brief messages, arch and sprightly. One, an invitation, is in ingenious verse—her favorite "8's" and "6's," but strung out in four long lines of "14-ers" to look like prose; the rhymes are only approximate, and there are no capital letters to set off the lines. (I have added slash marks to indicate verse divisions.)

> A little poem we will write / unto our Cousin John, / to tell him if he does not come / and see us very soon, / we will immediately forget / there's any such a man, / and when he comes to see us, / we will not be "at home."

Such fooling might lead one to write off the relationship as merely casual were it not for several other indications, one from an outside source and two from Emily herself. The first is Eliza Coleman's remark in a letter to Graves (October 4, 1854), cited earlier as a sign of the growing breach between Emily and the Amherst community. Here it shows that she was not without some understanding friends:

> *Emilie* . . . sends me beautiful letters & each one makes me love her more. I know you appreciate her & I think few of her Amherst friends do. They wholly misinterpret her, I believe—

Who these friends were who misinterpreted her, and what Eliza's evidence was, we would like to know, unless her remark is simply an indication of the general response of the community to Emily's increasingly offish attitude toward Amherst piety and good works. In such a situation a loyal and handsome cousin was good to have. About the time Eliza wrote to Graves, Emily wrote quite happily to Sue:

> Father and mother were gone last week, upon a little journey, and we rioted somewhat, like most ungodly children—John came down twice from Sunderland, to pass a day with us.

The two letters in which Emily put her heart out to John came toward the end of their association. He graduated with high honors in August 1855, giving the Philosophical Oration at Commencement (on "Philological Philosophy"). Next spring, in late April, Emily wrote him a letter of the sort we have seen paralleled in several of her early correspondences. It was tender, nostalgic, poetical—a little elegy on the end of things, strange in the April setting, but appropriate to what she saw, perhaps, as the end of their relationship. The day was Sunday, the family had gone to church. She set the scene (the Dickinsons were now in the house on Main Street, with its greater space and evergreen trees and "crumbling wall" that divided their land from the Sweetsers') and began to tell John what she saw from her vantage point and "what I would that you saw—" In the account, she seems to be reaching for a poem, or poems; details of the scene take on instant symbolism, the lyric impulse surges, and with the sentence beginning "Much that is gay," the language becomes metrical. The climax (in the final sentence, set off in a paragraph) shows her triumphing over the mortuary theme.

> You remember the crumbling wall that divides us from Mr Sweetser— and the crumbling elms and evergreens—and *other* crumbling things—that spring, and fade, and cast their bloom within a simple twelvemonth—well— *they and here,* and skies on me fairer far than Italy, in blue eye look down— up—see!—away—a league from here, on the way to Heaven! And here are Robins—just got home—and giddy Crows—and Jays—and will you trust me—as I live, here's a bumblebee—not such as summer brings—John— earnest, manly bees, but a kind of a Cockney, dressed in jaunty clothes. Much that is gay—have I to show, if you were with me, John, upon this April grass—then there are sadder features—here and there, wings half gone to dust, that fluttered so, last year—a mouldering plume, an empty house, in which a bird resided. Where last year's flies, their errand ran, and last year's crickets fell! We, too, are flying—fading, John—and the song "here lies," soon upon lips that love us now—will have hummed and ended.
>
> To live, and die, and mount again the triumphant body, and *next* time, try the upper air—is no schoolboy's theme!

That Emily did not attend church that morning with her family probably gained her no good will either from her family or from the congregation—one of the reasons, perhaps, for Eliza's concern about her being misinterpreted. Only John Graves could have known what she was up to. And few besides John (and Austin?) in Amherst would not have been shocked by the way she carried on (in the next passage of the letter) with a veritable burlesque of the Resurrection—and this during the Easter season:

> It is a jolly thought to think that we can be Eternal—when air and earth are *full* of lives that are gone—and done—and a conceited thing indeed, this promised Resurrection! *Congratulate* me—John—Lad—and "here's a health to *you*"—that we have each a *pair* of lives, and need not chary be, of the one "that *now* is"—
> Ha—ha—if any can afford—'tis *us* a roundelay!

The rest of the letter tapers off into nostalgia: "Mid your momentous cares [as schoolteacher in Orford, New Hampshire], pleasant to know that 'Lang Syne' has it's own place—" She speaks of "those triumphant days—Our April," the spring when she and Sue and John were alone in the Pleasant Street house, and she recalls one particularly haunting memory of those days, or rather nights, when she entertained John (and woke up Sue) with her piano.

If Newton was one of the very few to understand her poetic promise, John Graves was among the few who, of all her contemporaries who must have heard her play, has left on record his impression of her music, a major interest, especially in her early years, and one worth a brief comment. Many years later, his daughter wrote the following account of her father's visits with the Dickinsons:

> Oftentimes, during these visits to the Dickinson relatives, father would be awakened from his sleep by heavenly music. Emily would explain in the morning, "I can improvise better at night." On one or two occasions, when not under their friendly roof, my father, in paying his respects at the house, would receive a message from his cousin Emily, saying, "If you will stay in the next room, and open the folding doors a few inches, I'll come down to make music for you." My father said that in those early days she seemed like a will-o-the-wisp.[4]

Emily's letter describes one of those haunting moments:

> I play the old, odd tunes yet, which used to flit about your head after honest hours—and wake dear Sue, and madden me, with their grief and fun—How far from us, that spring seems—

This was not the only time she played for him, since John was often asked to spend the night in the Dickinson house when Mr. and Mrs. Dickinson were away. The tunes she played for John were apparently her own. She had outgrown the "beautiful pieces" she boasted to Abiah about learning when she was fourteen—"The Grave is Bonaparte," "Lancers Quick Step," and "Maiden Weep No More"—just as she was outgrowing (the parallel may not be too extravagant) the kind of poetry that was then in vogue. Her particular talent, it seems, was for improvising, and she did it better at night— a clue, perhaps, to her literary habits, since her letters often refer to her writing when all the others were asleep. (She wrote Austin on March 14, 1854: "Then I wrote a long letter to Father . . . then crept to bed softly, not to wake all the folks, who had been asleep a long time.")

At any rate, the nocturnal sessions that John was privileged to hear are of no little significance in what they tell us about her music and the part it played in her developing poetic career. In the early days she enjoyed most of the musical opportunities of the neighborhood. She took lessons in voice and piano. She heard Jenny Lind in Northampton in 1851 ("*Herself,* and not her music," she wrote Austin, "was what we seemed to love"); in 1853, Graves took her and Vinnie to a concert by the famous Germania Serenade Band, then on a national tour (she called them *"brazen Robins"*); she spoke of a pleasant meeting of the "girls 'Musical'" at her house in April 1853 and (perhaps) of being unable to attend another some six years later.

But all this time she was getting deeper and deeper into a music of a different sort. In her second letter to Higginson she wrote that "the noise in the Pool, at Noon—excels my Piano." As her practical interest in music declined, her metaphoric interest increased. In trying to capture in her poetry the "music" of nature, she put to use all she had learned about music as a child, and in college, and from the hymns she heard in church, whose metrical schemes were to become her chosen and all but exclusive form.[5] At a crucial point in her career, her "business," she said, was to *"sing"*; she wished for her nephew's sake that the Bible had a "warbling Teller"; she asked the Norcross cousins, during a time of bereavement, to "Let Emily sing for you because she cannot pray"—all metaphors that grew out of a lifetime's association with the thing itself. She had shifted from the old music to the new, but the old lived on as part of her poetry.

A poem of about 1860 shows the change. All the early part is here— the hymns, carrying the "treble" in the choirs at the Academy and Mount Holyoke, even the Germania Band in full regalia. But the poem concerns another kind of music:

> Musicians wrestle everywhere—
> All day—among the crowded air
> I hear the silver strife—

And—waking—long before the morn—
Such transport breaks upon the town
I think it that "New life"!

It is not Bird—it has no nest—
Nor "Band"—in brass and scarlet—drest—
Nor Tamborin—nor Man—
It is not Hymn from pulpit read—
The "Morning Stars" the Treble led
On Time's first Afternoon!

Some—say—it is "the Spheres"—at play!
Some say—that bright Majority
Of vanished Dames—and Men!
Some—think it service in the place
Where we—with late—celestial face—
Please God—shall Ascertain!   (#157)

Even the hint of ambivalence in her reminiscence to John Graves about the old tunes that "maddened" her is present here in the "wrestling" musicians and the "silver strife," a motif which recurs in many phrases and figures in her later writing. In 1873 the pianist Anton Rubinstein made her think of "polar nights," and in a poem of about 1879 she wrote of "The fascinating chill that music leaves." In the poem "There's a certain Slant of light," the light of the sun on the landscape late winter afternoons "oppresses, like the Heft / Of Cathedral Tunes—" Once she remarked to Higginson that the change of the seasons "hurt almost like Music—shifting when it ease us most." Curiously, the words "melody" or "harmony" usually had no such association for her; but "music" *hurt*. It may not be too farfetched to say that in her poetry she found a medium more viable in a quite literal sense. She could live with it—it was her true medium, as music was not, no matter how "heavenly" her music sounded to the appreciative John Graves.[6]

But the "triumphant days" and the musical evenings were soon over. After graduation and several years of teaching at Orford Academy, where he married Frances Britton on September 1, 1858, Graves studied for the ministry and was ordained pastor of a new Congregational church in Boston on January 4, 1860. He soon gave it up and went into business. When Edward Dickinson died suddenly in Boston in 1874, Graves came to Amherst to help with the family and give what information he could about the circumstances of the death. If he saw Emily and talked with her, there is no record of it. His daughter wrote that whenever he spoke of her in later years "there was about him a kind of glow," and he would say, "unlike anyone else—a grace, a charm . . ."

What she thought about him, how deep her feeling went, can only be conjectured. A hint that it was more than casual is in her last, or next-to-last, letter to him (the date is uncertain).[7] It is a brief note and may have been written well before he left Amherst. It may have arisen from some minor contretemps and thus have been partly playful. Or, as with many of her early friendships about this time, it may have meant the end.

NOTES

[1] On January 23, 1850, Emily wrote to Jane Humphrey (*L* I, 84): "I had a letter—and Ralph Emerson's Poems—a beautiful copy—from Newton the other day. I should love to read you them both—they are very pleasant to me. I can write him in about three weeks— and I *shall*."

[2] *L* II, 404 (April 25, 1862). Leyda (*YH* I, liv) thinks it likely that Emily was referring to Jacob Holt, a student in Amherst Academy in the early 1840s who had come to practice dentistry in Amherst in August 1845 after a period of study and practice in Boston. He had published several verses in the *Northampton Courier* that Emily must have seen. His health was poor, and Emily inquired about him three times in letters to Austin from Mount Holyoke. He died of tuberculosis on May 14, 1848, and was memorialized by some verses in the *Hampshire and Franklin Express* for May 18. On June 8 the *Express* printed "the following brief but expressive lines written by Dr. Holt during his sickness:"

THE BIBLE

'Tis a pure and holy word,
'Tis the wisdom of a God,
'Tis a fountain full and free,
'Tis the Book for *you* and *me;*
'Twill the soul's best anchor be
Over life's tempestuous sea,
A guardian angel to the tomb,
A meteor in the world's dark gloom;
'Tis a shining sun at even,
'Tis a *diamond dropt from heaven.*

Emily copied the poem on the back leaf of her Bible and pasted an obituary notice beside it (*YH* 1, 147). Whether it was Ben Newton or Jacob Holt who taught Emily Dickinson immortality is a question that may never be answered with certainty. It may be worth pointing out that the "friend" mentioned in the letter to Higginson is pretty clearly the same as "My dying Tutor" of the next letter to Higginson (*L* II, 408; June 7, 1862). There is no record of any association with Holt such as Emily enjoyed with Newton, who had been "much in our family." The *Express* for May 18, 1848, says that Holt was twenty-six when he died (*YH* I, 144), which would make him eight years Emily's senior.

³ The MS of this letter, recently discovered in Hale's papers, is in the Lilly Library, University of Indiana, and is printed here by permission.

⁴ *YH* I, 301–2. The quotation is from an article by Gertrude M. Graves in the Boston *Sunday Globe,* January 12, 1930. See *L* I, 19 n.: "No reliable account of her playing has been preserved, though Mrs. Bianchi recorded [*Emily Dickinson Face to Face,* p. 157] her mother's memory of ED's improvisations." Just how musical she was (*Home,* p. 153) is "hard to say. . . . One [Clara Newman Turner; cf. Appendix II, 3] who heard her strange, limited repertoire said that before seating herself at the piano Emily covered the upper and lower octaves so that the length of the keyboard might correspond to that of the old-fashioned instrument on which she had learned to play." At least twice, in later years, she asked friends to sing for her (Nora Green and Mabel Todd) and listened to them, in her odd way, from upstairs (*YH* II, 273, 357). Kate Scott Anthon, in a letter to Martha Bianchi, October 8, 1917, recalled those "blissful evenings at Austin's" (in the late 1850s) when Emily was "often at the piano playing weird & beautiful melodies, all from her own inspiration . . ." (*YH* I, 367).

⁵ For ED's use of the hymn meters, see Thomas H. Johnson, *Emily Dickinson: An Interpretive Biography,* pp. 84 ff. Copies of Isaac Watt's *Christian Psalmody* and *The Psalms, Hymns, and Spiritual Songs* were in Edward Dickinson's library. David T. Porter, *The Art of Emily Dickinson's Early Poetry* (1966), p. 55, speaks of her lifelong use of hymn meters as "a constant occasion for irony," as she used the orthodox form to express unorthodox views. (He discusses the subject at length in his fourth chapter.) Leonard Conversi brought to my attention the similar practice of Thomas Hardy, who used "Common Measure" (as John Crowe Ransom points out) for heretical poems: "There are no churches, nor hymns, which will embody or publish Hardy's peculiar views." Ransom speculates on Hardy's early experience of the hymns, in many ways applicable to ED's: "Hardy would have known it [the common measure] very well from the many hymns he had sung as a youth. Their tunes lingered nostalgically in his mind even after he had lost his faith, and we find him writing poems about them. At any rate, the scruple of good workmanship shows just as clearly in hymnology as in architecture; and in the visual and aural versions of a poem as in the meaningful" (*Selected Poems of Thomas Hardy,* 1961, pp. xiv–xv). "Common Measure" (or Meter) is the "8's" and "6's" referred to above.

⁶ That, at a certain point, she made a professional decision about music is suggested in Clara Bellinger Green's memory of her conversation with ED after Nora Green sang for her: "She told us of her early love for the piano and confided that, after hearing Rubinstein [?]— I believe it was Rubinstein—play in Boston, she had become convinced that she could never master the art and had forthwith abandoned it once and for all, giving herself up then wholly to literature" (*YH* II, 273).

⁷ *L* II, 330. Here, on the basis of the handwriting, the conjectured date is "about 1856," and the letter printed *after* the "Lang Syne" letter. *YH* I, 327, however, suggests mid-January 1855 as the date and prints it well *before* the "Lang Syne" letter, juxtaposing it with the "box of Phantoms" letter to Sue. But neither the handwriting nor the duplication of phrasing can be regarded as conclusive. At best, the evidence of the handwriting is imprecise within a year or so, and frequently ED used similar phrases in letters and poems years apart. I print the shorter letter last because we know that, historically, the friendship did come to an end about this time (although Graves never lost touch with the Dickinsons and cherished his memory of Emily). The shorter letter can stand, at least symbolically, as a *Hic finis est.*

JUDY JO SMALL

A Musical Aesthetic
(1990)

As a teenager, Dickinson wrote to a friend, "you know how I hate to be common" (L 5). The statement is a telling one, for it marks a trait in her temperament that proved to be permanent: cultivation of an elite self defiant of conventional authority. Her deliberate separation from the common would extend to stylistic revision of traditional practices of the literary establishment. Her peculiar rhymes in particular are part of a "fuller tune" that she set out to give to the sounds of poetry.

> I shall keep singing!
> Birds will pass me
> On their way to Yellower Climes—
> Each—with a Robin's expectation—
> I—with my Redbreast—
> And my Rhymes—
>
> Late—when I take my place in summer—
> But—I shall bring a fuller tune—
> Vespers—are sweeter than Matins—Signor—
> Morning—only the seed of Noon—
>
> (P 250)

This poem is something of a poetic manifesto, and its phrasing emphasizes the poet's awareness of herself as belated, part of a poetic process active long before her arrival. Whatever anxiety she may have felt with regard to her precursor poets, however, the tone here betrays no sense of impotence; on the contrary, with a mock-deferential bow to "Signor," she expresses confident assurance that she will bring a superior fullness to the tradition. Significantly, as she does again and again, she speaks of poetry as music, as song, and she expresses her revisionary intent in musical terms.

Much has been written about Emily Dickinson's visual and visionary power; the power of her auditory imagination, however, has been relatively neglected. The prominence in her poetry of sound and music, both as content and as acoustic texture, merits far more attention. Her poems often rely on auditory images and aural figures referring to metaphysical concepts. She writes repeatedly about the effects of sound on the hearer. And her poems and letters indicate not only that she had a keen auditory sensitivity but also that she had given thought to the ways sound conveys meaning. Her ideas about sound and about music hold implications relevant to her handling of sound devices in poetry and specifically to her uncommon handling of rhyme.

"*My* business is to *sing*," she wrote to her friends the Hollands (L 269). In the context of her letter, the statement, attributed to a bird that has been singing in her garden, stands as part of a parable with meaning immediately applicable to her writing a second letter when her previous one had received no answer. Her statement also must have had, at least for Dickinson, meaning applicable to her dedication to a poetic career, particularly since she wrote the letter some time in or around 1862, at about the same time she wrote to Higginson the more famous and cryptic statement "My Business is Circumference" (L 268). Much earlier, in 1850, struggling with a temptation that seemed irreligious, she had written to Jane Humphrey: "The path of duty looks very ugly indeed—and the place where *I* want to go more amiable—a great deal—it is so much easier to do wrong than right—so much pleasanter to be evil than good, I dont wonder that good angels weep—and bad ones sing songs" (L 30). Even then, she seems to have been thinking of her real vocation as a kind of singing.

Writing to Higginson for artistic guidance, she wonders, "Could you tell me how to grow—or is it unconveyed—like Melody—or Witchcraft?" (L 261). In the same letter, she confesses, "I had a terror—since September—I could tell to none—and so I sing, as the Boy does by the Burying Ground—because I am afraid—." To her Norcross cousins she writes some time after the death of Elizabeth Barrett Browning, "I noticed that Robert Browning had made another poem, and was astonished—till I remembered that I, myself, in my smaller way, sang off charnel steps" (L 298). She asks in one poem,

> Why—do they shut Me out of Heaven?
> Did I sing—too loud?
>
> (P 248)

She thought of herself as a singer, and it is no coincidence that her poetry is full of singing birds, which often carry metaphorical value relevant to artistic expression. She frequently describes herself as like a bird—a wren (L 268), a phoebe (P 1009), a bobolink (L 223), or, as in "I shall keep singing," quoted above, a robin.

In depicting herself as a songbird, Dickinson is aligning herself with the contemporary female poets, who were commonly referred to as little birds sweetly chirping spontaneous lays.[1] Not only female poets were regarded as singers—the metaphor is an ancient one, of course, and derives from the time when poetry and song were in fact one art. Dickinson's linking of herself and Robert Browning as singers makes it clear that she by no means considered herself as part of an exclusively female tradition. Nevertheless, when she adopts the stance of a simple songbird singing either sweetly or "too loud," she evokes the standard image of the nineteenth-century poetess, a distorted image with which Dickinson has often been mistakenly identified. Though indeed her writing should be viewed in the context of a flourishing subculture of women writing and publishing popular lyrics, it is important not to lose sight of the fact that Dickinson's uses of gender stereotypes are frequently subversive.

Caroline May's *The American Female Poets* (1869) is a representative treasury of the clichés current about women who wrote poetry and thus of what might be called "the songbird tradition." In the preface, May says appreciatively, "poetry, which is the language of the affections, has been freely employed among us to express the emotions of woman's heart." The profusion of women's verse in periodical literature, she says, unwittingly deprecating the product she praises, "has led many to underrate the genuine value, which upon closer examination will be found appertaining to these *snatches* of American song" (v) [emphasis added]. Of Caroline Gilman she writes: "Her poems are unaffected and sprightly; inspired by warm domestic affection, and pure religious feeling" (115). Of Sarah Louisa P. Smith: "The qualities of her heart were superior to those of her head; and bright as the shining intellect was, the lustre of her love and truth and purity far outshone it . . . ; and when we are assured that to beauty, genius, and amiability, there was added the most ardent and unaffected piety, we may well believe that she was fitted while on earth for singing among the seraphs in heaven" (298). Of Lydia Jane Peirson: "Her privations and inconveniences were many, and her sorrows, too; but she poured out her soul in song, and found—to use her own words—that her 'converse with poetry, wild-flowers, and singing birds, was nearly all that made life endurable'" (303). Of Catherine H. Esling: "Her poems are smoothly and gracefully written; always pleasing, from the deep and pure affection they display. . . . [She never] left her home for a greater distance than forty miles, or for a longer period than forty-eight hours. Well may such a nestling bird sing sweetly of home's quiet joys!" (328). And of Amelia B. Welby: "her rhythm is always correct, and always full of melody, worthy of expressing the ardent impulses of a true and guileless heart. Pure friendship, undivided admiration for the beautiful, and ever-gushing love for the gifts of loving Nature, seem to be the chief incentives to her song" (471). The composite picture of these poets is indistinguishable from that offered by Henry Coppee in his introduction to *A Gallery of Distinguished English and American Female Poets* (1860): ". . . from secluded homes, from the midst of household duties,—woman's truest *profession*,—the daughters of song send forth, bird-like, sweet heart-melodies, which can no more be restrained than the voice of the morning lark, or the plaintive sounds of the nightingale" (xv). Obviously, the image of Dickinson in legend and in popular perception bears more than a passing resemblance to the nineteenth-century idea of the "female poet."

The disparity between this debased image of the woman poet and the real lives of women who wrote and struggled to have their works regarded seriously has become increasingly evident through feminist scholarship in recent years.[2] Dickinson was influenced by the writings of female poets, but she appropriated the stereotyped image of the female poet for her own ends. In her study of American women's poetry, *Nightingale's Burden*, Cheryl Walker has identified a number of poetic subjects that Dickinson derived from that women's tradition—"the concern with intense feeling, the ambivalence toward power, the fascination with death, the forbidden lover and secret sorrow" (116). She might have added, as her title implies, the sweet bird pouring out her heart's joys and pains in melody. For Walker shrewdly observes that Dickinson "toyed in her poems with that stock character the poetess, craftily using the conventions of the role to serve her own purposes and then rewriting the part to suit herself" (87). That is precisely what happens when Dickinson takes up the role of the songbird.

In that role, as so often happens in her self-presentations, "what looks like demurral, reticence, and self-abnegation can also be interpreted as a stubborn assertion of self-importance" (Juhasz 35). While the songbird metaphor types the woman writer as guileless, instinctive, scarcely conscious of matters of art (except, perhaps, correctness of rhythm), Dickinson is only *apparently* the guileless warbler, pouring forth her soul artlessly. She is, at least in part, posing. When she writes of the motives for song, she is drawing upon the tradition: sometimes a song is a way to use the idle time of life's waiting and "To Keep the Dark away" (P 850), sometimes it is a remedy for pain (P 755), and sometimes it is just "For Extasy—of it" (P 653) or "for joy to Nobody" but one's own "seraphic self" (P 1465). Elsewhere, when she ponders *why* a bird sings—"to earn the Crumb" (P 880) or not to earn the crumb (P 864), she makes more original use of the conventional subjects but remains within the tradition; the actual question, surely, is whether public recognition and remuneration should or should not be part of a poet's aim, an issue of considerable concern to women writers, who were not supposed to care about such things. But when she sings too loud and with mock remorse offers to sing "a little 'Minor' / Timid as a Bird" (P 248), she is standing the tradition on its head, parodically offering to mimic the timid little songs of timid little poetesses who do their best not to trouble the gentlemen who control the gateways to power. And when she decides (P 324) to "keep the Sabbath" not at church but in her own backyard "With a Bobolink for a Chorister" and another little bird for a "Sexton," she uses the conventional role of the female poet as home-loving and sensitive to nature while at the same time flouting the sentimental piety conventionally associated with the role. When she, artfully artless, daringly constructs irregular rhythms and eccentric rhymes that seem to have gushed willy-nilly from a simple heart, she reshapes the whole idea of verse melodies, bringing in fact "a fuller tune."

Lydia Huntley Sigourney was known as the "Sweet Singer of Hartford." Lydia Jane Pierson was called "the forest minstrel." Dickinson too set out to be a singer, but—hating to be common—a singer of a superior sort. In "I cannot dance upon my Toes," she exults in her ability as poet-musician.

> I cannot dance upon my Toes—
> No Man instructed me—
> But oftentimes, among my mind,
> A Glee possesseth me,
>
> That had I Ballet knowledge—
> Would put itself abroad
> In Pirouette to blanch a Troupe—
> Or lay a Prima, mad,
>
> And though I had no Gown of Gauze—
> No Ringlet, to my Hair,
> Nor hopped for Audiences—like Birds,
> One Claw upon the Air,
>
> Nor tossed my shape in Eider Balls,
> Nor rolled on wheels of snow
> Till I was out of sight, in sound,
> The House encore me so—
>
> Nor any know I know the Art
> I mention—easy—Here—
> Nor any Placard boast me—
> It's full as Opera—

(P 326)

As Anderson points out, the phrase "A Glee possesseth me" refers to min-
strelsy and hence to bardic inspiration (23). More immediate to Dickinson's
experience, though, were popular songs called "glees" and the glee clubs,
popular in towns throughout America, such as existed at Amherst College.
In this poem, all the balletic details are a surface decoration deflecting at-
tention, like an epic simile, from the poem's main concern, for she says this
"Glee," that is, this song in her mind that is also her joy, *would* express itself
in ballet but *does* not because she has no gown, no ballet steps, no ballet
knowledge—we may remark the string of negatives. The "Art" she knows
and practices "out of sight, in sound" (and why else would she use this
phrase?) is the "Glee," the art of poetic song, and at this art she is a virtuoso
and knows it, proclaiming "gleefully," "It's full as Opera."

As a singer of glees, as bobolink, as robin, as wren, Dickinson exploits the
songbird convention of contemporary female poetry, then, but her refer
ences to song and music should be seen in relation to a broader historical
context as well, the general interest of the nineteenth century in the music
of poetry. Of Dickinson's immediate forebears, Edgar Allan Poe had focused
attention on the musical aspect of poetry; in the preface to his *Poems* of 1831,
he argued that the object of poetry is "an *indefinite* instead of a *definite* plea-
sure . . . to which end music is an *essential,* since the comprehension of sweet
sound is our most indefinite conception. Music, when combined with a
pleasurable idea, is poetry . . ." ("Letter" 17). Poe's theories were to influence
the French symbolist poets, whose aesthetic stressed the suggestive nuance,
the melody of language: "De la musique avant toute chose," Verlaine's "Art
poétique" declared (326)—"Music before everything." Emerson's essay "The
Poet" claimed that "whenever we are so finely organized that we can pene-
trate into that region where the air is music, we hear those primal warblings
and attempt to write them down . . ." (5–6). Earlier, Thomas Carlyle
(whose portrait Dickinson kept on her wall) had written in his discussion of
the hero as poet, "A *musical* thought is one spoken by a mind that has pene-
trated into the inmost heart of the thing; detected the inmost mystery of
it, namely the *melody* that lies hidden in it; the inward harmony of coher-
ence which is its soul . . . (108–9). See deep enough, and you see musically,
the heart of Nature *being* everywhere music, if you can only reach it. . . ."
Sidney Lanier wrote a treatise probing the links between verse and music,
The Science of English Verse. Walt Whitman found poetic inspiration in the
opera. The association of music with sublimity permeated the age. Music,
as Joseph Kerman says, "became the paradigmatic art for the Romantics be-
cause it was the freest, the least tied down to earthly manifestations such as
representation in painting and denotation in literature" (65). Walter Pater's

pronouncement in *The Renaissance* that "[a]ll art constantly aspires towards the condition of music" (106) must not be thought extravagant: it merely articulates an aesthetic belief then very widely held.[3]

Twentieth-century theorists have tended to recoil from the Romantic fascination with the music of poetry. When Irving Babbitt discussed the turning away of Romantic poets from the classical doctrine of *ut pictura poesis* towards musical suggestiveness, his essay became a diatribe against confusion of the arts, warning that "The constant menace that hangs over the whole ultra-impressionistic school is an incomprehensible symbolism" (185, 169). Such criticism has been profoundly influential, to the extent that many students of literature have become contemptuous of discussions of the "music of poetry" and uncomfortable even with discussions of the sound of poetry, which can seem all too subjective. The relationship of sound and meaning is admittedly a murky area. It is not yet clear to what extent the mere sound of a word, beyond the level of onomatopoeia, can be said to convey meaning at all. Since sounds do not have correspondent meanings in any universal system of signification, either musical or linguistic, talk about "the music of poetry," based on a dubious analogy, is unscientific and can indeed seem impressionistic. René Wellek and Austin Warren have held that "[t]he term 'musicality' (or 'melody') of verse should be dropped as misleading. The phenomena we are identifying are not parallel to musical 'melody' at all . . ." (159).

Still, I would like to urge, Dickinson shared the Romantic concern with the ineffable power of music; further, it is precisely because music and sound generally are so indefinite in their suggestiveness, so resistant to analysis, that she found them appealing. Music, she wrote, "suggests to our Faith" rather than to "our Sight," which must be "put away" (P 797).[4] Like other Romantic writers, she criticized the cast of mind that, demanding certainty, is stupidly insensitive to sublimity. Logical analysis quickly becomes a murderous dissection, for example, in this satirical poem:

> Split the Lark—and you'll find the Music—
> Bulb after Bulb, in Silver rolled—
> Scantily dealt to the Summer Morning
> Saved for your Ear when Lutes be old.

> Loose the Flood—you shall find it patent—
> Gush after Gush, reserved for you—
> Scarlet Experiment! Sceptic Thomas!
> Now, do you doubt that your Bird was true?

(P 861)

As it so often does in her poetry, "Music" here represents the elusive sublime. The "Sceptic," whose doubt in the presence of the miraculous links him in shame with the disciple who demanded to touch the wounds of the resurrected Christ, is determined to probe and pry until he locates the song of the lark. The song, though, is impalpable, not contained in the physical mechanism of the bird's body, and it cannot be separated from the secret of its life. Remembering Dickinson's frequent presentations of herself as a poetic songbird, the analyst of her poetry may find in this poem a warning against improper skepticism. Her first letter to Higginson besought him to tell her if her poetry was "alive," if it "breathed." Together, the abundance of her musical references and the persistence of her uncommon phonetic practices argue that she knew that "Music" was part of the vital life of her poetry.

NOTES

[1]   For this idea I am indebted to Mary G. De Jong and her paper "Frances Osgood, Sara Helen Whitman, and 'The Poetess.'"

[2]   Ann D. Wood, considering the "scribbling women" of the nineteenth century, discusses the popular descriptions of women writing "heedless of any sense of literary form," from "instinctive womanly nature," "because they cannot help it." At the origin of such descriptions, she explains, was a taboo against competition by women, especially economic competition in the marketplace: "women's motives in writing are being stripped [by these descriptions] of all aggressive content" (18–19).

[3]   M. H. Abrams discusses the importance of music in the expressive theory of aesthetics in *The Mirror and the Lamp*, 91–94.

[4]   This poem, about the pine at her window which the wind rushes through, ends "Apprehensions—are God's introductions— / To be hallowed—accordingly." The poem may owe something to Emerson's "Woodnotes," which also associates the wind with the breath of the primal mind.

ALLEN TATE

Emily Dickinson
(1932)

Great poetry needs no special features of difficulty to make it mysterious. When it has them, the reputation of the poet is likely to remain uncertain. This is still true of Donne, and it is true of Emily Dickinson, whose verse appeared in an age unfavorable to the use of intelligence in poetry. Her poetry is not like any other poetry of her time; it is not like any of the innumerable kinds of verse written today. In still another respect it is far removed from us. It is a poetry of ideas, and it demands of the reader a point of view—not an opinion of the New Deal or of the League of Nations, but an ingrained philosophy that is fundamental, a settled attitude that is almost extinct in this eclectic age. Yet it is not the sort of poetry of ideas which, like Pope's, requires a point of view only. It requires also, for the deepest understanding, which must go beneath the verbal excitement of the style, a highly developed sense of the specific quality of poetry—a quality that most persons accept as the accidental feature of something else that the poet thinks he has to say. This is one reason why Miss Dickinson's poetry has not been widely read.

There is another reason, and it is a part of the problem peculiar to a poetry that comes out of fundamental ideas. It exalted more and more the personal and the unique in the interior sense. Where the old-fashioned puritans got together on a rigid doctrine, and could thus be individualists in manners, the nineteenth-century New Englander, lacking a genuine religious center, began to be a social conformist. The common idea of the Redemption, for example, was replaced by the conformist idea of respectability among neighbors whose spiritual disorder, not very evident at the surface, was becoming acute. A great idea was breaking up, and society was moving towards external uniformity, which is usually the measure of the spiritual sterility inside.

At this juncture Emerson came upon the scene: the Lucifer of Concord, he had better be called hereafter, for he was the light-bearer who could see nothing but light, and was fearfully blind. He looked around and saw the uniformity of life, and called it the routine of tradition, the tyranny of the theological idea. The death of Priam put an end to the hope of Troy, but it was a slight feat of arms for the doughty Pyrrhus; Priam was an old gentleman and almost dead. So was theocracy; and Emerson killed it. In this way he accelerated a tendency that he disliked. It was a great intellectual mistake. By it Emerson unwittingly became the prophet of a piratical industrialism, a consequence of his own transcendental individualism that he could not foresee. He was hoist with his own petard.

He discredited more than any other man the puritan drama of the soul. The age that followed, from 1865 on, expired in a genteel secularism, a mildly didactic order of feeling whose ornaments were Lowell, Longfellow, and Holmes. "After Emerson had done his work," says Mr. Robert Penn Warren, "any tragic possibilities in that culture were dissipated." Hawthorne alone in his time kept pure, in the primitive terms, the primitive vision; he brings the puritan tragedy to its climax. Man, measured by a great idea outside himself, is found wanting. But for Emerson man is greater than any idea and, being himself the Over-Soul, is innately perfect; there is no struggle because—I state the Emersonian doctrine, which is very slippery, in its extreme terms—because there is no possibility of error. There is no drama in human character because there is no tragic fault. It is not surprising, then, that after Emerson New England literature tastes like a sip of cambric tea. Its center of vision has disappeared. There is Hawthorne looking back, there is Emerson looking not too clearly at anything ahead: Emily Dickinson, who has in her something of both, comes in somewhere between.

With the exception of Poe there is no other American poet whose work so steadily emerges, under pressure of certain disintegrating obsessions, from the framework of moral character. There is none of whom it is truer to say that the poet *is* the poetry. Perhaps this explains the zeal of her admirers for her biography; it explains, in part at least, the gratuitous mystery that Mrs. Bianchi, a niece of the poet and her official biographer, has made of her life. The devoted controversy that Miss Josephine Pollitt and Miss Genevieve Taggard started a few years ago with their excellent books shows the extent to which the critics feel the intimate connection of her life and work. Admiration and affection are pleased to linger over the tokens of a great life; but the solution to the Dickinson enigma is peculiarly superior to fact.

The meaning of the identity—which we merely feel—of character and poetry would be exceedingly obscure, even if we could draw up a kind of Binet correlation between the two sets of "facts." Miss Dickinson was a recluse; but her poetry is rich with a profound and varied experience. Where did she get it? Now some of the biographers, nervous in the presence of this discrepancy, are eager to find her a love affair, and I think this search is due to a modern prejudice: we believe that no virgin can know enough to write poetry. We shall never learn where she got the rich quality of her mind. The moral image that we have of Miss Dickinson stands out in every poem; it is that of a dominating spinster whose very sweetness must have been formidable. Yet her poetry constantly moves within an absolute order of truths that overwhelmed her simply because to her they were unalterably fixed. It is dangerous to assume that her "life," which to the biographers means the thwarted love affair she is supposed to have had, gave to her poetry a decisive direction. It is even more dangerous to suppose that it made her a poet.

Poets are mysterious, but a poet when all is said is not much more mysterious than a banker. The critics remain spellbound by the technical license of her verse and by the puzzle of her personal life. Personality is a legitimate interest because it is an incurable interest, but legitimate as a personal interest only; it will never give up the key to anyone's verse. Used to that end, the interest is false. "It is apparent," writes Mr. Conrad Aiken, "that Miss Dickinson became a hermit by deliberate and conscious choice"—a sensible remark that we cannot repeat too often. If it were necessary to explain her seclusion with disappointment in love, there would remain the discrepancy between what the seclusion produced and the seclusion looked at as a cause. The effect, which is her poetry, would imply the whole complex of anterior fact, which was the social and religious structure of New England.

The problem to be kept in mind is thus the meaning of her "deliberate and conscious" decision to withdraw from life to her upstairs room. This simple fact is not very important. But that it must have been her sole way of acting out her part in the history of her culture, which made, with the variations of circumstance, a single demand upon all its representatives—this is of the greatest consequence. All pity for Miss Dickinson's "starved life" is misdirected. Her life was one of the richest and deepest ever lived on this continent.

When she went upstairs and closed the door, she mastered life by rejecting it. Others in their way had done it before; still others did it later. If we suppose—which is to suppose the improbable—that the love-affair precipitated the seclusion, it was only a pretext; she would have found another. Mastery of the world by rejecting the world was the doctrine, even if it was not always the practice, of Jonathan Edwards and Cotton Mather. It is the meaning of fate in Hawthorne: his people are fated to withdraw from the world and to be destroyed. And it is one of the great themes of Henry James.

There is a moral emphasis that connects Hawthorne, James, and Miss Dickinson, and I think it is instructive. Between Hawthorne and James lies an epoch. The temptation to sin, in Hawthorne, is, in James, transformed into the temptation not to do the "decent thing." A whole world-scheme, a complete cosmic background, has shrunk to the dimensions of the individual conscience. This epoch between Hawthorne and James lies in Emerson. James found himself in the post-Emersonian world, and he could not, without violating the detachment proper to an artist, undo Emerson's work; he had that kind of intelligence which refuses to break its head against history. There was left to him only the value, the historic role, of rejection. He could merely escape from the physical presence of that world which, for convenience, we may call Emerson's world: he could only take his Americans to Europe upon the vain quest of something that they had lost at home. His characters, fleeing the wreckage of the puritan culture, preserved only their honor. Honor became a sort of forlorn hope struggling against the forces of "pure fact" that had got loose in the middle of the century. Honor alone is a poor weapon against nature, being too personal, finical, and proud, and James achieved a victory by refusing to engage the whole force of the enemy.

In Emily Dickinson the conflict takes place on a vaster field. The enemy to all those New Englanders was Nature, and Miss Dickinson saw into the character of this enemy more deeply than any of the others. The general symbol of Nature, for her, is Death, and her weapon against Death is the entire powerful dumb-show of the puritan theology led by Redemption and Immortality. Morally speaking, the problem for James and Miss Dickinson is similar. But her advantages were greater than his. The advantages lay in the availability to her of the puritan ideas of the theological plane.

These ideas, in her poetry, are momently assailed by the disintegrating force of Nature (appearing as Death) which, while constantly breaking them down, constantly redefines and strengthens them. The values are purified by the triumphant withdrawal from Nature, by their power to recover from Nature. The poet attains to a mastery over experience by facing its utmost implications. There is the clash of powerful opposites, and in all great poetry—for Emily Dickinson is a great poet—it issues in a tension between abstraction and sensation in which the two elements may be, of course, distinguished logically, but not really. We are shown our roots in Nature by examining our differences with Nature; we are renewed by Nature without being delivered into her hands. When it is possible for a poet to do this for us with the greatest imaginative comprehension, a possibility that the poet cannot himself create, we have the perfect literary situation. Only a few times in the history of English poetry has this situation come about, notably, the period between about 1580 and the Restoration. There was a similar age in New England from which emerged two talents of the first order— Hawthorne and Emily Dickinson.

There is an epoch between James and Miss Dickinson. But between her and Hawthorne there exists a difference of intellectual quality. She lacks almost radically the power to seize upon and understand abstractions for their own sake; she does not separate them from the sensuous illuminations that she is so marvelously adept at; like Donne, she *perceives abstraction* and *thinks sensation*. But Hawthorne was a master of ideas, within a limited range; this narrowness confined him to his own kind of life, his own society, and out of it grew his typical forms of experience, his steady, almost obsessed vision of man; it explains his depth and intensity. Yet he is always conscious of the abstract, doctrinal aspect of his mind, and when his vision of action and emotion is weak, his work becomes didactic. Now Miss Dickinson's poetry often runs into quasi-homiletic forms, but it is never didactic. Her very ignorance, her lack of formal intellectual training, preserved her from the risk that imperiled Hawthorne. She cannot reason at all. She can only *see*. It is impossible to imagine what she might have done with drama or fiction; for, not approaching the puritan temper and through it the puritan myth, through human action, she is able to grasp the terms of the myth directly and by a feat that amounts almost to anthropomorphism, to give them a luminous tension, a kind of drama, among themselves.

One of the perfect poems in English is "The Chariot," and it illustrates better than anything else she wrote the special quality of her mind. I think it will illuminate the tendency of this discussion:

Because I could not stop for death,
He kindly stopped for me;
The carriage held but just ourselves
And immortality.

We slowly drove, he knew no haste,
And I had put away
My labor, and my leisure too,
For his civility.

We passed the school where children played,
Their lessons scarcely done;
We passed the fields of gazing grain,
We passed the setting sun.

We paused before a house that seemed
A swelling of the ground;
The roof was scarcely visible,
The cornice but a mound.

Since then 'tis centuries; but each
Feels shorter than the day
I first surmised the horses' heads
Were toward eternity.

If the word great means anything in poetry, this poem is one of the greatest in the English language. The rhythm charges with movement the pattern of suspended action back of the poem. Every image is precise and, moreover, not merely beautiful, but fused with the central idea. Every image extends and intensifies every other. The third stanza especially shows Miss Dickinson's power to fuse, into a single order of perception, a heterogeneous series: the children, the grain, and the setting sun (time) have the same degree of credibility; the first subtly preparing for the last. The sharp *gazing* before *grain* instills into nature a cold vitality of which the qualitative richness has infinite depth. The content of death in the poem eludes explicit definition. He is a gentleman taking a lady out for a drive. But note the restraint that keeps the poet from carrying this so far that it becomes ludicrous and incredible; and note the subtly interfused erotic motive, which the idea of death has presented to most romantic poets, love being a symbol interchangeable with death. The terror of death is objectified through this figure of the genteel driver, who is made ironically to serve the end of Immortality. This is the heart of the poem: she has presented a typical Christian theme in its final irresolution, without making any final statements about it. There is no solution to the problem; there can be only a presentation of it in the full context of intellect and feeling. A construction of the human will, elaborated with all the abstracting powers of the mind, is put to the concrete test of experience: the idea of immortality is confronted with the fact of physical disintegration. We are not told what to think; we are told to look at the situation.

The framework of the poem is, in fact, the two abstractions, mortality and eternity, which are made to associate in equality with the images: she sees the ideas, and thinks the perceptions. She did, of course, nothing of the sort; but we must use the logical distinctions, even to the extent of paradox, if we are to form any notion of this rare quality of mind. She could not in the proper sense think at all, and unless we prefer the feeble poetry of moral ideas that flourished in New England in the eighties, we must conclude that her intellectual deficiency contributed at least negatively to her great distinction. Miss Dickinson is probably the only Anglo-American poet of her century whose work exhibits the perfect literary situation—in which is possible the fusion of sensibility and thought. Unlike her contemporaries, she never succumbed to her ideas, to easy solutions, to her private desires.

Philosophers must deal with ideas, but the trouble with most nineteenth-century poets is too much philosophy; they are nearer to being philosophers than poets, without being in the true sense either. Tennyson is a good example of this; so is Arnold in his weak moments. There have been poets like Milton and Donne, who were not spoiled for their true business by leaning on a rational system of ideas, who understood the poetic use of ideas. Tennyson tried to mix a little Huxley and a little Broad Church, without understanding either Broad Church or Huxley; the result was fatal, and what is worse, it was shallow. Miss Dickinson's ideas were deeply imbedded in her character, not taken from the latest tract. A conscious cultivation of ideas in poetry is always dangerous and even Milton escaped ruin only by having an instinct for what in the deepest sense he understood. Even at that there is a remote quality in Milton's approach to his material, in his treatment of it; in the nineteenth century, in an imperfect literary situation where literature was confused with documentation, he might have been a pseudo-philosopher-poet. It is difficult to conceive Emily Dickinson and John Donne succumbing to rumination about "problems"; they would not have written at all.

Neither the feeling nor the style of Miss Dickinson belongs to the seventeenth century; yet between her and Donne there are remarkable ties. Their religious ideas, their abstractions, are momently toppling from the rational plane to the level of perception. The ideas, in fact, are no longer the impersonal religious symbols created anew in the heat of emotion, that we find in poets like Herbert and Vaughan. They have become, for Donne, the terms of personality; they are mingled with the miscellany of sensation. In Miss Dickinson, as in Donne, we may detect a singularly morbid concern, not for religious truth, but for personal revelation. The modern word is self-exploitation. It is egoism grown irresponsible in religion and decadent in morals. In religion it is blasphemy; in society it means usually that culture is not self-contained and sufficient, that the spiritual community is breaking up. This is, along with some other features that do not concern us here, the perfect literary situation.

II

Personal revelation of the kind that Donne and Miss Dickinson strove for, in the effort to understand their relation to the world, is a feature of all great poetry; it is probably the hidden motive for writing. It is the effort of the individual to live apart from a cultural tradition that no longer sustains him. But this culture, which I now wish to discuss a little, is indispensable: there is a great deal of shallow nonsense in modern criticism which holds that poetry—and this is a half-truth that is worse than false—is essentially revolutionary. It is only indirectly revolutionary: the intellectual and religious background of an age no longer contains the whole spirit, and the poet proceeds to examine that background in terms of immediate experience. But the background is necessary; otherwise all the arts (not only poetry) would have to rise in a vacuum. Poetry does not dispense with tradition; it probes the deficiencies of a tradition. But it must have a tradition to probe. It is too bad that Arnold did not explain his doctrine, that poetry is a criticism of life, from the viewpoint of its background: we should have been spared an era of academic misconception, in which criticism of life meant a diluted pragmatism, the criterion of which was respectability. The poet in the true sense "criticizes" his tradition, either as such, or indirectly by comparing it with something that is about to replace it; he does what the root-meaning of the verb implies—he *discerns* its real elements and thus establishes its value, by putting it to the test of experience.

What is the nature of a poet's culture? Or, to put the question properly, what is the meaning of culture for poetry? All the great poets become the material of what we popularly call culture; we study them to acquire it. It is clear that Addison was more cultivated than Shakespeare; nevertheless Shakespeare is a finer source of culture than Addison. What is the meaning of this? Plainly it is that learning has never had anything to do with culture except instrumentally: the poet must be exactly literate enough to write down fully and precisely what he has to say, but no more. The source of a poet's true culture lies back of the paraphernalia of culture, and not all the historical activity of an enlightened age can create it.

A culture cannot be consciously created. It is an available source of ideas that are imbedded in a complete and homogeneous society. The poet finds himself balanced upon the moment when such a world is about to fall, when it threatens to run out into looser and less self-sufficient impulses. This world order is assimilated, in Miss Dickinson, as medievalism was in Shakespeare, to the poetic vision; it is brought down from abstraction to personal sensibility.

In this connection it may be said that the prior conditions for great poetry, given a great talent, may be reduced to two: the thoroughness of the poet's discipline in an objective system of truth, and his lack of consciousness of such a discipline. For this discipline is a number of fundamental ideas the origin of which the poet does not know; they give form and stability to his fresh perceptions of the world; and he cannot shake them off. This is his culture, and like Tennyson's God it is nearer than hands and feet. With reasonable certainty we unearth the elements of Shakespeare's culture, and yet it is equally certain—so innocent was he of his own resources—that he would not know what our discussion is about. He appeared at the collapse of the medieval system as a rigid pattern of life, but that pattern remained in Shakespeare what Shelley called a "fixed point of reference" for his sensibility. Miss Dickinson, as we have seen, was born into the equilibrium of an old and a new order. Puritanism could not be to her what it had been to the generation of Cotton Mather—a body of absolute truths; it was an unconscious discipline timed to the pulse of her life.

The perfect literary situation: it produces, because it is rare, a special and perhaps the most distinguished kind of poet. I am not trying to invent a new critical category. Such poets are never very much alike on the surface; they show us all the varieties of poetic feeling; and like other poets they resist all classification but that of temporary convenience. But, I believe, Miss Dickinson and John Donne would have this in common: their sense of the natural world is not blunted by a too rigid system of ideas; yet the ideas, the abstractions, their education or their intellectual heritage, are not so weak as to let their immersion in nature, or their purely personal quality, get out of control. The two poles of the mind are not separately visible; we infer them from the lucid tension that may be most readily illustrated by polar activity. There is no thought as such at all; nor is there feeling; there is that unique focus of experience which is at once neither and both.

Like Miss Dickinson, Shakespeare is without opinions; his peculiar merit is also deeply involved in his failure to think about anything; his meaning is not in the content of his expression; it is in the tension of the dramatic relations of his characters. This kind of poetry is at the opposite of intellectualism. (Miss Dickinson is obscure and difficult, but that is not intellectualism.) To T. W. Higginson, the editor of *The Atlantic Monthly,* who tried to advise her, she wrote that she had no education. In any sense that Higginson could understand, it was quite true. His kind of education was the conscious cultivation of abstractions. She did not reason about the world she saw; she merely saw it. The "ideas" implicit in the world within her rose up, concentrated in her immediate perception.

That kind of world at present has for us something of the fascination of a buried city. There is none like it. When such worlds exist, when such cultures flourish, they support not only the poet but all members of society. For, from these, the poet differs only in his gift for exhibiting the structure, the internal lineaments, of his culture by threatening to tear them apart: a process that concentrates the symbolic emotions of society while it seems to attack them. The poet may hate his age; he may be an outcast like Villon; but this world is always there as the background to what he has to say. It is the lens through which he brings nature to focus and control—the clarifying medium that concentrates his personal feeling. It is ready-made; he cannot make it; with it, his poetry has a spontaneity and a certainty of direction that, without it, it would lack. No poet could have invented the ideas of "The Chariot"; only a great poet could have found their imaginative equivalents. Miss Dickinson was a deep mind writing from a deep culture, and when she came to poetry, she came infallibly.

Infallibly, at her best; for no poet has ever been perfect, nor is Emily Dickinson. Her precision of statement is due to the directness with which the abstract framework of her thought acts upon its unorganized material. The two elements of her style, considered as point of view, are immortality, or the idea of permanence, and the physical process of death or decay. Her diction has two corresponding features: words of Latin or Greek origin and, sharply opposed to these, the concrete Saxon element. It is this verbal conflict that gives to her verse its high tension; it is not a device deliberately seized upon, but a feeling for language that senses out the two fundamental components of English and their metaphysical relation: the Latin for ideas and the Saxon for perceptions—the peculiar virtue of English as a poetic language.

Like most poets Miss Dickinson often writes out of habit; the style that emerged from some deep exploration of an idea is carried on as verbal habit when she has nothing to say. She indulges herself:

> There's something quieter than sleep
> Within this inner room!
> It wears a sprig upon its breast,
> And will not tell its name.
>
> Some touch it and some kiss it,
> Some chafe its idle hand;
> It has a simple gravity
> I do not understand!
>
> While simple hearted neighbors
> Chat of the "early dead,"
> We, prone to periphrasis,
> Remark that birds have fled!

It is only a pert remark; at best a superior kind of punning—one of the worst specimens of her occasional interest in herself. But she never had the slightest interest in the public. Were four poems or five published in her lifetime? She never felt the temptation to round off a poem for public exhibition. Higginson's kindly offer to make her verse "correct" was an invitation to throw her work into the public ring—the ring of Lowell and Longfellow. He could not see that he was tampering with one of the rarest literary integrities of all time. Here was a poet who had no use for the supports of authorship—flattery and fame; she never needed money.

She had all the elements of a culture that has broken up, a culture that on the religious side takes its place in the museum of spiritual antiquities. Puritanism, as a unified version of the world, is dead; only a remnant of it in trade may be said to survive. In the history of puritanism she comes between Hawthorne and Emerson. She has Hawthorne's matter, which a too irresponsible personality tends to dilute into a form like Emerson's; she is often betrayed by words. But she is not the poet of personal sentiment; she has more to say than she can put down in any one poem. Like Hardy and Whitman she must be read entire; like Shakespeare she never gives up her meaning in a single line.

She is therefore a perfect subject for the kind of criticism which is chiefly concerned with general ideas. She exhibits one of the permanent relations between personality and objective truth, and she deserves the special attention of our time, which lacks that kind of truth.

She has Hawthorne's intellectual toughness, a hard, definite sense of the physical world. The highest flights to God, the most extravagant metaphors of the strange and the remote, come back to a point of casuistry, to a moral dilemma of the experienced world. There is, in spite of the homiletic vein of utterance, no abstract speculation, nor is there a message to society; she speaks wholly to the individual experience. She offers to the unimaginative no riot of vicarious sensation; she has no useful maxims for men of action. Up to this point her resemblance to Emerson is slight: poetry is a sufficient form of utterance, and her devotion to it is pure. But in Emily Dickinson the puritan world is no longer self-contained; it is no longer complete; her sensibility exceeds its dimensions. She has trimmed down its supernatural proportions; it has become a morality; instead of the tragedy of the spirit there is a commentary upon it. Her poetry is a magnificent personal confession, blasphemous and, in its self-revelation, its honesty, almost obscene. It comes out of an intellectual life towards which it feels no moral responsibility. Cotton Mather would have burnt her for a witch.

HENRY W. WELLS

Romantic Sensibility
(1947)

The contrasted seeds of mysticism and Stoicism took root in Emily's mind not only because of her own personality, but through a congenial ground prepared for them by romantic sensibility. From a remote past ultimately came the two of her most precious heritages. But from her own cultural age she prudently drew what it had best to give. In view of her total accomplishments she is neither a mystic nor a stoic poet, though she undeniably is both mystical and stoical. Neither can her total achievement be labelled or confined by such descriptive epithets as classical, romantic, or modern. In some degree answering to each specification, her total stature can best be described in the phrase shrewdly noted by her biographer: "this was a poet." Nevertheless for a rounded appreciation of her art, recognition of its definitely romantic quality is essential, since no major aspect of her work can be properly grasped while others are disregarded. Her mind was integrated at least to the extent that such qualities as her peculiar mysticism and Stoicism are themselves properly explained only in the light of her romantic environment and soul.

Just as it is true that Emily remains far from wholly romantic, so it is clear that the whole of Romanticism in the historical sense is not to be traced in her own work. Singularly free from many of the qualities of her contemporaries or immediate predecessors, she has little specifically in common with the romantic poets, either of her own time of Tennyson, Browning, Swinburne, and Arnold, or the earlier period of Wordsworth, Coleridge, Keats, and Shelley. That she revolted from a Calvinistic training which she could never wholly forget, by no means makes her a follower of Byron, whose thought thus far, at least, followed hers. That she devoured Scott's tales, in no way allied her creative mind to the acknowledged master of the early nineteenth-century novel. She well knew that she followed her own star. Yet the popularity of her poems when first published, far surpassing the expectations of her editors and publishers, proves her to have been in some respects indigenous to her age. The woman who confessed that, whether with or against her will, she perforce saw "New Englandly," must have known that she also saw to some extent in the light of her age, coincident with the height of the Romantic Movement. Her conscious aims to retain the fresh imagination of childhood, to celebrate the self, to praise nature, and to indulge freely in fancy, stood among the most conspicuous ideals in the literature of her century. Although in the last analysis both her spirit and her style break violently with leading cultural patterns of the century, she was still its child, however naughty and rebellious. In no respect did she comply more closely than in cultivating the richest and most conspicuous vein in romantic thought as a whole, namely the new sensibility.

This sensibility is a mental state both in life and art accentuating the emotional life. Under circumstances which would at any time evoke strong feelings, romantic theory and practice made them still stronger; under conditions which would hardly be expected to elicit emotional responses at all, this sensibility begot an ample flow of sentiment. To the romantics, feeling became a badge of distinction, just as in the Restoration world "wit" was so regarded. Artifice became social practice, or, in Oscar Wilde's words, life imitated art. The familiar story requires no retelling here, but should be at least recalled. Women kneaded their emotions into a refined state of sensitivity, while men affected effeminacy. Soft phrases and melting airs grew to be marks of polite society. It was ingeniously contrived to man's temporary comfort and lasting discomfort that as industrial society grew uglier the personal life grew more refined. This hyperdevelopment of purely personal reactions accompanied the rise of revolutionary individualism and *laissez faire* at the same time that it soothed the old or more conservative regimes into a forgetfulness of social ills known only too well. Radicals and conservatives differed on almost all scores save one, but in that one respect happily concurred. Virtually all men and women loved the poem or novel of sentiment. Sensibility was the cultural slogan of the age. The man of feeling became the man of distinction. Whereas Aristotle, arch-master of the classically minded, advocated the stern elimination of piety and fear, romantic leaders in poetry and fiction founded their art upon a shameless exploitation of these very emotions. Sympathy and terror ruled the imagination of the Revolutionary Age, and even governed much of its practice. Sympathizing with the conditions of the poor, revolutionaries aimed to relieve their poverty and reduce the hard inequalities of opportunity. Conservatives found social utility in focussing in private life the emotionalism indulged by the reformers in their attitudes toward society. Both dwelt with fond sorrow over their own misfortunes. Art and literature evolved into a vast hyperbole of passion; effeminacy, or at best a literature more appropriate to the feminine boudoir than the masculine forum, gained ascendency; sentimental clichés distorted style; in time it grew even more fashionable to pity one's self than to pity the poor; and, finally, with so many forced, affected, and abnormal attitudes disfiguring a fundamentally morbid society, neurotic elements tyrannized in art and poetry, and very nearly dominated all fields of aesthetic expression. Shelley's career perfectly represents the usual course traversed by the romantic author, and—what is more important—epitomizes the evolution of the entire movement. He began by pitying the poor and ended by pitying himself.

All these too-well-known qualities, for better and for worse, inevitably leave some marks on Emily's verse. Though never sentimental to the degree of hypocrisy, nor extravagant to that of vulgarity, she utilizes her age for the best interests of her art, and occasionally commits the inevitable mistakes. In no other period, perhaps, could her writing have acquired such warmth; in none could it have fallen victim to the peculiar lapses which at times prevent it from attaining greatness.

Certain passages are the most conspicuous in betokening her romantic background. A number of her poems offer particularly apt illustration of the romantic tendency to indulge an hyperbole of emotionalism. "Dare you see a soul at the white heat?" is, for example, a lyric admirably in key with its first line. There is a touch of self-consciousness here, not as yet precisely a weakness, but indicative of the true romantic spirit. Certain of Emily's verses show a keen awareness of the physical states of the body induced by extremes of nervous excitement. They are paralleled by her account of true

poetry itself, which, as told to the incredulous Colonel Higginson, she iden-
tified as an experience making her "feel physically as though the top of my
head were taken off." Her verse abounds in trembling, freezing, and burn-
ing. The following is indicative:

> It was not frost, for on my flesh
> I felt siroccos crawl,—
> Nor fire, for just my marble feet
> Could keep a chancel cool.

The verse of this tightly restrained New Englander contains many images
drawn from volcanic fires. Significantly enough, volcanoes fascinated and
haunted her. Their "reticent" ways, periodically giving place to violent irrup-
tion, paralleled her own experiences and the behavior of her friends and
family.

> A crater I may contemplate,
> Vesuvius at home.

One commentator has somewhat boldly equated this Vesuvius with the
outbreaks of her father's anger. Although some of her most moving love po-
ems are majestically impersonal, or, in other words, come near to Sappho or
Dante than to Browning or Tennyson, a number by no means of her least
impressive pieces are stamped with marks of peculiarly romantic sensibility.
One of her best known lyrics, "Although I put away his life," is very much
in Mrs. Browning's equally sentimental and realistic manner. Emily dreams
of a connubial happiness that has failed to be realized. She might have been
the faithful and devoted servant of a husband, sowing the flowers he pre-
ferred, soothing his pains, pushing pebbles from his path, playing his fa-
vorite tunes, or fetching him his slippers. The more fanciful of her love
hyperboles also tend to follow current patterns. One of her longest lyrics, "I
cannot live with you," proves a more concise version of the romantic theme
of love and immortality as handled in Rossetti's *Blessed Damosel*. Emily
vividly describes her own sensitivity in language unmistakably romantic, as
when she asks the rhetorical question why a bird at daybreak

> Should stab my ravished spirit
> With dirks of melody.

She is even critical of her own romantic excesses. In finely romantic diction
she voices the fear that her lines may drip overmuch and have too red a glow:

> Sang from the heart, Sire,
> Dipped my beak in it.

If the tune drip too much,
Have a tint too red,

Pardon the cochineal,
Suffer the vermilion,
Death is the wealth
Of the poorest bird,

Without losing high merit, Emily's verse occasionally steps down from a high and impersonal dignity to assume the consciously feminine manner especially admired in the mid-nineteenth century. Though the poetry is more than commonplace it is less than universal. The feminine note grows unmistakable. This is heard most clearly in the poem describing a girl's excitement on receiving a message from her lover: "The way I read a letter's thus." In a manner which Samuel Richardson would have approved, she tells how she locks the door, fingers the envelope, glances nervously about to assure herself of absolute privacy, and, finally, reads the words of a lover whose identity she coyly declines to disclose. "I am ashamed, I hide," describes in some detail a bride's bashfulness according to the most familiar romantic ideals. "Wert thou but ill," similarly describes the bride who romantically protests that she will follow her lover through a series of the most trying misfortunes. Much of the sentiment in Emily's nature poetry also betrays the age of sensibility. This shows clearly in a little poem, "To lose, if one can find again." The poet tenderly covers over her garden, hopefully awaiting springtime resurrection, as she confidently expects reunion in heaven with her beloved.

Even though Emily never descends to the baser moods of self-pity, it would be superficial to overlook the romantic poignance which her verses occasionally attain through a tendency in this perilous direction. "I was the slightest in the house," she writes, in an autobiographical poem somewhat exaggerating her own social limitations. With similar self-consciousness she addresses herself as, "the favorite of doom." "Don't put up my thread and needle," she writes, in a tender and genuine piece descriptive of her own hopes and fears in time of dangerous sickness. In several of her poems, as the notable, "'Twas just this time last year I died," she indulges the melancholy fancy that she is dead, and wonders how gravely or how lightly the family will cherish her memory. Such poetry affords a nice contrast to the same theme treated in the witty and cynical Augustan manner in Swift's remarkable lines, *On the Death of Dean Swift*.

After the unabashed fashion of romantic poets, Emily at times unhesitatingly exposes the more neurotic features of her personality. Such writing falls into the emphatically self-conscious romantic idiom. With powerful imagery she describes the gingerly walk of the neurotic genius through the terrifying jungles of experience: "I stepped from plank to plank." She discloses the painful tensions within the pathological soul. In one poem, "The body grows outside," she describes the soul as hiding behind the flesh. In another, "Me from Myself to banish," she reveals the agonies of the split personality, pains of which she must herself have been poignantly aware. Briefly, at least, she probes the tragic abyss of her own sub-conscious: "The subterranean freight, The cellars of the soul." In a tragic poem, "Had we our senses," she suggests that men would become even madder if they saw clearly into their own madness. Sanity is merely the integument of an invincible stupidity. Baudelaire himself could have proposed no more cynical a view.

These various romantic attitudes Emily shares and explores, without as a rule falling victim to the typical banalities of her times, either in meaning or expression. In other words, her poetry shares the deeper and grander qualities of her chief contemporaries without sinking for any length of time into the commonplaces of romantic thought, sentiment, and style. In this regard it becomes appropriate to note a few instances in which her language or her images come close to losing the sharpness and distinction of her own literary personality. "Glee! the great storm is over!," for instance, approximates the style of the typical, undistinguished romantic ballad. The rhymes are commonplace: "land—sand"; "souls—shoals"; "door—more"; "eye—reply." The meter is painfully regular. The symbols of sailors shipwrecked or saved hardly achieve distinction. Longfellow himself might have written the final line: "And only the waves reply." The poem has a saving irony which is Emily's own and preserves it from bathos; but it remains extremely romantic. Another lyric, "Good night! which put the candle out?" is comprised of a series of all-too-familiar romantic images drawn from home or the sea. In still another, "Forever cherished be the tree," the image of two robins as two angels has the customary nineteenth-century extravagance with little assurance of Emily's better genius. In short, to her contacts with the Romantic Age she owed a small but very definite part of her artistic success; and much the greater part of her by no means fatal faults. Her devotion to "eternity" may have been due in part to a distrust, at times latent and at times highly conscious, of the dominating fashions of her times. Although she distrusted Romanticism, she was too shrewd to discard it altogether.

Sample Student Research Paper

Lavery 1

Rachel Lavery

American Literature

Professor M. Halio

7 July 1997

"The Musicality of

Emily Dickinson's Poetry"

Because Emily Dickinson's poetry is musical,
it lends itself readily to adaptations by compos-
ers. In the twentieth century, many of her poems
and even her letters have been set to music. Some
have been scored by more than one composer, and
her verse has been intriguing to composers as
varied as traditionalist Aaron Copland and mini-
malist John Adams.

In her critical essay "A Musical Aesthetic,"
Judy Jo Small examines the parts of Dickinson's
life that may have contributed to the musicality
of her poems. Small cites Dickinson's piano play-
ing from an early age, her immersion in hymns, and
her desire to sing, which Dickinson wrote about
in several poems and letters to friends (72).
Small contends that Dickinson wrote poetry at
least partly to fulfill this desire to express
herself musically. According to Small, "Signifi-
cantly, as she does again and again, she speaks
of poetry as music, as song, and she expresses
her revisionary intent in musical terms" (72).
Clearly, Dickinson intended her poetry to be
musical; therefore, it is not surprising that
twentieth-century adaptations of her work by
composers have enriched her verse.

Thesis statement

Lavery 2

Small contends that Dickinson "thought of herself as a singer" (73). Certainly, from a very early age, Dickinson was immersed in music. At the age of two, she played the piano. Later she studied voice at a singing school, and in her teenage years she practiced piano two hours a day. Small argues that "Dickinson may once have had serious musical ambitions that she relinquished for poetry" (73), but she nevertheless managed to carry her love for music into her poetry. Her work contains echoes of hymns and nursery rhymes; she has frequent references to harmony, and she often uses music as a metaphor for beauty.

Expert opinion in support of Dickinson's "musicality"

Richard Sewall, her primary biographer, cites many examples of Dickinson's speaking of singing, and surrounding herself in music:

Expert opinion in support of Dickinson's "musicality"

> In trying to capture in her poetry the 'music' of nature, she put to use all she had learned about music as a child, and in college, and from the hymns she heard in church, whose metrical schemes were to become her chosen and all but exclusive form. (Sewall 68)

Sewall continues, "[Her] metaphors . . . grew out of a lifetime's association with the thing itself," (68) meaning music. He cites the many critics who have commented on the influence of church hymns on her poetry, especially hymns

Lavery 3

written by Isaac Watts. Like Small, Sewall con-
tends that Dickinson was quite serious about her
piano playing, at least until she heard the fa-
mous Anton Rubinstein play (69).

In addition to meter and metaphor, Dickinson
uses word choice and punctuation to give her po-
etry a musical quality. The "melody" of her po-
etry can have many different characteristics.
For example, her punctuation can make a line more
staccato (crisp, sharp). Dashes also create a
staccato feel. Lack of punctuation, words heavy
with vowels and particularly the letter s give a
legato feel (smoothness) to a line. Single words,
such as eternity, can have their own rhythm, and
when the words combine vowels with stop-plosives,
such as t and d, and fricatives such as f and v,
they have a staccato beat.

Dickinson uses all of these techniques in
one of her most famous poems, "Because I could
not stop for Death" (#712). For example, Dickin-
son produces a carried-over legato line where
she uses no punctuation:

. . . He knew no haste
And I had put away
my labor and my leisure too . . .

The complete line is very musical; instinctively,
a singer knows to draw the line out, to extend
the sound to mirror the feeling of taking one's
time. Throughout the poem, Dickinson also uses
l words or multisyllabic words to contribute

Discussion of musical terms Dickinson uses in her poems

Example of Dickinson's use of musical techniques

Lavery 4

to the legato of the line--for example, <u>labor</u>, <u>leisure</u>, <u>civility</u>, <u>gazing</u>, <u>setting</u>, <u>gossamer</u>, <u>swelling</u>, <u>cornices</u>, and <u>scarcely</u>. Where Dickinson adds punctuation--especially the famous dashes-- a more staccato-like line is created, as when she interrupts herself with a line such as "Or rather--He passed us--."

Allen Tate calls "Because I could not stop for Death" "one of the greatest [poems] in the English language" (84). He says, "The rhythm charges with movement the pattern of suspended action back of the poem. Every image is precise and, moreover, not merely beautiful, but fused with the central idea (84).

> Transitional paragraph introducing adaptations by Copland and Adams

Two very different American composers, Aaron Copland and John Adams, adapted this poem to music by thinking of the poem's images in different ways. When Aaron Copland adapted "Because I could not stop for Death" to music with the title "The Chariot," he used the musical aspects of Dickinson's poem as inspiration and added features of his own. Ironically, he created a hauntingly light-hearted setting for a poem that focuses on death. The piece begins with a succession of sixteenth then dotted eighth notes, creating a bouncy rhythm that gives it almost a happy quality. As the grave comes into view ("We paused before a swelling of the ground"), the dynamic marking is <u>mezzo piano</u> (rather soft) and "calm." As the music moves into a description of the

> Musical adaptation: Copland

Lavery 5

grave, ("The roof was scarcely visible . . ."),
it is marked <u>mezzo forte</u>, or moderately loud.
Copland seems to want the singer to realize this
is <u>her</u> grave, because the very next bar becomes
musically darker. "Since then 'tis centuries" is
marked <u>mezzo forte</u> and "a trifle broader." This
is the high moment of the piece, and the music
does not quiet until a decrescendo (decrease in
loudness) beginning at "horse's heads," then be-
coming piano (soft) at "toward eternity," which
is sung on a high F as if the sound itself were

Be-cause I   would not stop for Death, ———

EX. 1. Aaron Copland, <u>Eight Poems of Emily Dickinson</u>.
(New York: Boosey and Hawkes, 1970) 90.

Musical
illustrations are
labeled *example.*
Other types of
illustrations are
labeled *figure.*

floating away toward eternity in a gentle car-
riage ride.

Copland's interpretation of the poem seems
to fit with what Dickinson herself intended. In
"Because I could not stop," Dickinson is asking
"What does it feel like to die?" She imagines a
slow-paced carriage ride with a most civil part-
ner, Death, who "kindly" stops for her. They
ride past children at recess, past "Fields of
Gazing Grain," and finally, the atmosphere grow-
ing chillier, come to the grave, the "Swelling
of the Ground." It is the end of the long day of
dying, and thoughts turn to what eternity must
be. Copland treats the text musically with child-

Lavery 6

like wonder and an exploration of death that seem
appropriate to Dickinson's words.

John Adams's interpretation of the same poem
is very different from Copland's more traditional
work. His score is also calm, but it is not cheer-
ful. It consists of a lush, choral sound made by
a choir of men and women who sing through the
poem in a semi-chant. Their voices rise a bit
and hold on "Immortality," also repeated. At the
word "civility," which is also repeated, the
key changes from minor to major, brightening
the mood. The music grows, and with a background
of strings becomes darker again, until the words
are no longer intelligible.

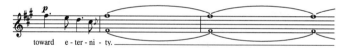

toward e - ter - ni - ty.

EX. 2. Aaron Copland, <u>Eight Poems of Emily Dickinson</u>.
(New York: Boosey and Hawkes, 1970) 101.

From the beginning crescendo, brass droning
underneath the music gives it a climactic feel-
ing. At the approach to the Grave, the words are
no longer intelligible, masked by the crescendo
(increase in volume) and swell in brass and
voices. "'Tis centuries" is once again calm, the
men singing the verse with the sopranos "oohing"
underneath. The ending is placid and sounds fi-
nal, as the men fade into eternity and the women
"ooh" like calling angels, similar to the mood of
Copland's conclusion.

Lavery 7

It seems that Copland in his score views the poem as an actual trip, a journey toward a final destination--death. His calling his piece "The Chariot" is significant. In Copland, the music moves along with the journey, but Adams sets up each scene as a tableau with chant-like singing and repeating, then moves on to the next scene. He builds each picture then refocuses, becoming climactic. There are small eruptions of forte (loud).

Another example of Dickinson's poetry that has been set to music is "Wild Nights!" It is easy to see why composers would be interested in adapting this poem. From the very first line, "Wild Nights--Wild Nights!" Dickinson uses words of one syllable with a dash in between and an exclamation point at the end to make the words scream and sing: "Were I with thee/Wild Nights would be our luxury!" The legato line followed by the capitalized "Wild Nights" and an exclamation point creates a staccato effect.

Musical adaptation: Adam's "Wild Nights"

When Adams adapted this controversial poem to music, he added significantly to its exotic, sexual energy, which on paper seems bold and sexual. In the beginning stanza, the speaker-author seems to be in the throes of passion. Low strings vibrate like a boat moving through the sea, timpani grows louder, finally fading into fast string; the brass crescendo with urgency, the bells explode, the sopranos enter, anxiously, shrilly, belting "Wild Nights!" By the third

stanza of the poem, the speaker-author seems more
content and in the musical setting the orgasmic
quality is even more apparent. The instrumental
prelude with the fast string instruments, omi-
nous brass, and andante bells give the listener
a feeling for the poem's urgent sexuality. The
screaming sopranos bring the instruments to a
frenzied climax that lasts throughout the rest
of the poem.

Would Dickinson have approved of setting her
work to music in this way? The confines of the
period in which she lived would not have allowed
the sort of music that Copland and Adams com-
posed. However, the frenzied passion of their
musical scores reflects the heart, desire, and
music of Dickinson's verse.

Dickinson's possible reaction to composers

For twentieth-century readers who encounter
"Wild Nights" not knowing anything about the au-
thor, the sexuality is easy to see, but is not
shocking (as it was to Victorian readers). After
learning about Dickinson and her life of sexual
denial, the poem becomes more intriguing, and
Adams's interpretation fascinating. This recluse,
in her room writing passionately, had paper rela-
tionships with men, none of which resulted in
marriage. The working of her imagination--a tryst
with a longed-for lover--is vivid on paper, but
it is even more vivid in the Adams setting.
This adaptation is a good example of music giv-
ing the words more power than they originally
had. But each reinforces the other: at first

Discussion of music's enrichment of poetry

Lavery 9

hearing, Adams's music may not sound very me-
lodic, but a knowledge of Dickinson's life en-
riches the music--and the music makes the poem
very powerful.

Dickinson's intellect and passion came at
a time when women were not encouraged to give
voice to feelings of sexuality. Her verse, like
music, came soaring out of her. Unfortunately,
Dickinson believed the ears of her time would
not hear her song, so she put her music into her
verse where it could be heard by later genera-
tions of readers. Often she questioned her effect
on her audience, asking, "Why--do they shut me
out of heaven? Did I sing--too loud?"

Conclusion--
reinforces
thesis

Lavery 10
Works Cited

Halio, Marcia Peoples, ed. <u>Emily Dickinson: A Collection of Poems</u>. The Harcourt Brace Casebook Series in Literature. Fort Worth: Harcourt, 1998.

Sewall, Richard B. "Early Friendships." Halio 61-71.

Small, Judy Jo. "Excerpt from A Musical Aesthetic." Halio 72-79.

Tate, Allen. "Emily Dickinson." Halio 79-90.

Bibliography

Editions of the Poetry and Letters

Franklin, R. W., ed. *The Manuscript Books of Emily Dickinson,* 2 vols. Cambridge: Harvard UP, 1981.

————. *The Master Letters of Emily Dickinson.* Amherst: Amherst College Press, 1986.

————. *The Poems of Emily Dickinson.* A variorum edition. Cambridge: Harvard UP, forthcoming.

Johnson, Thomas H., ed. *The Poems of Emily Dickinson: Including Variant Readings Critically Compared with All Known Manuscripts.* Cambridge: Belknap Press of Harvard UP, 1955.

Johnson, Thomas H. and Theodora Ward, eds. *The Letters of Emily Dickinson.* Cambridge: Harvard UP, 1958.

Pollak, Vivian, ed. *A Poet's Parents: The Courtship Letters of Emily Norcross and Edward Dickinson.* Chapel Hill: U of North Carolina P, 1988.

Sewall, Richard B., ed. *The Lyman Letters: New Light on Emily Dickinson and Her Family.* Amherst: U of Massachusetts P, 1965.

Todd, Mabel Loomis and Millicent Todd Bingham, eds. *Bolts of Melody: New Poems of Emily Dickinson.* NY: Harper and Brothers, 1945.

Todd, Mabel Loomis and T. W. Higginson, eds. *Poems by Emily Dickinson.* Boston: Roberts Brothers, 1896.

Chronology

Leyda, Jay. *The Years and Hours of Emily Dickinson.* New Haven: Yale UP, 1960.

Biographies

Bianchi, Martha Dickinson. *Emily Dickinson Face to Face: Unpublished Letters with Notes and Reminiscences.* Boston: Houghton Mifflin, 1932.

Bingham, Millicent Todd. *Ancestors' Brocades: The Literary Debut of Emily Dickinson.* New York: Harper & Brothers, 1945.

Johnson, Thomas H. *Emily Dickinson: An Interpretive Biography.* Cambridge: Harvard UP, 1955.

Longsworth, Polly. *Emily Dickinson: Her Letter to the World.* New York: Thomas Y. Crowell, 1965.

Sewall, Richard B. *The Life of Emily Dickinson.* 3 vols. New York: Farrar, Straus and Giroux, 1974.

Whicher, George Frisbie. *This Was a Poet: A Critical Biography of Emily Dickinson.* New York: Charles Scribner's Sons, 1938. Introd. Richard B. Sewall. Hamden: The Shoe String Press, Archon Books, 1980.

Wolff, Cynthia Griffin. *Emily Dickinson.* New York: Alfred A. Knopf, 1986.

PSYCHOLOGICAL BIOGRAPHIES

Cody, John. *After Great Pain: The Inner Life of Emily Dickinson.* Cambridge: Belknap Press of Harvard University, 1971.

Garbowsky, Maryanne M. *The House without the Door: A Study of Emily Dickinson and the Illness of Agoraphobia.* Cranbury: Association of University Presses, 1989.

Gelpi, Albert. *Emily Dickinson: The Mind of the Poet.* Cambridge: Harvard UP, 1966.

Mossberg, Barbara Antonina Clarke. *Emily Dickinson: When a Writer Is a Daughter.* Bloomington: Indiana UP, 1982.

GENERAL CRITICISM

Aiken, Conrad. *Collected Criticism of Conrad Aiken: A Reviewer's ABC.* Greenwich: Meridan Books, 1958.

Anderson, Charles R. *Emily Dickinson's Poetry: Stairway of Surprise.* New York: Holt, Rinehart & Winston, 1960.

Benfey, Christopher E. G. *Emily Dickinson and the Problem of Others.* Amherst: U of Massachusetts P, 1984.

Blake, Caesar R. and Carlton F. Wells, eds. *The Recognition of Emily Dickinson.* Ann Arbor: U of Michigan P, 1964.

Bloom, Harold, ed. *Emily Dickinson: Modern Critical Views.* New York: Chelsea House, 1985.

Buckingham, Willis J. *Emily Dickinson's Reception in the 1890s: A Documentary History.* Pittsburgh: U of Pittsburgh P, 1989.

Budick, E. Miller. *Emily Dickinson and the Life of Language: A Study in Symbolic Poetics.* Baton Rouge: Louisiana State UP, 1985.

Cady, Edwin H. and Louis J. Budd, eds. *On Dickinson: The Best from American Literature.* Durham, NC: Duke UP, 1990.

Cameron, Sharon. *Lyric Time: Dickinson and the Limits of Genre.* Baltimore: The Johns Hopkins UP, 1979.

———. *Choosing Not Choosing: Dickinson's Fascicles.* Chicago: U of Chicago P, 1992.

Capps, Jack L. *Emily Dickinson's Reading: 1836–1886.* Cambridge: Harvard UP, 1966.

Dandurand, Karen. "Another Dickinson Poem Published in Her Lifetime." *American Literature* 54 (1982): 434–37.

———. "New Dickinson Civil War Publications." *American Literature* 56 (1984): 17–27.

Diehl, Joanne Feit. *Dickinson and the Romantic Imagination.* Princeton: Princeton UP, 1981.

Dobson, Joanne. "'Compound Manner': Emily Dickinson and the Metaphysical Poets." In *On Dickinson.* Durham: Duke UP, 1990.

Eberwein, Jane Donahue. *Dickinson: Strategies of Limitation.* Amherst: U of Massachusetts P, 1985.

Farr, Judith, ed. *Emily Dickinson: A Collection of Critical Essays.* Englewood Cliffs: Prentice-Hall, 1996.

———. *The Passion of Emily Dickinson.* Cambridge: Harvard UP, 1992.

Ferlazzo, Paul J., ed. *Critical Essays on Emily Dickinson.* Boston: G. K. Hall and Co., 1984.

Franklin, R. W. *The Editing of Emily Dickinson: A Reconsideration.* Madison: U of Wisconsin P, 1967.

———. "The Emily Dickinson Fascicles." *Studies in Bibliography* 36 (1983): 1–20.

Gelpi, Albert. *The Tenth Muse.* Cambridge: Harvard UP, 1975.

Griffith, Clark. *The Long Shadow: Emily Dickinson's Tragic Poetry.* Princeton: Princeton UP, 1964.

Hagenbuchle, Roland. "Precision and Indeterminacy in Emily Dickinson's Poetry," *ESQ* 20.2 (1974): 33–56.

Higgins, David. *Portrait of Emily Dickinson: The Poet and Her Prose.* New Brunswick: Rutgers UP, 1967.

Howe, Susan. *My Emily Dickinson.* Berkeley: North Atlantic Books, 1985.

———. "Some Notes on Visual Intentionality in Emily Dickinson." *HOW(ever)* 3.4 (1986): 11–13.

———. "These Flames and Generosities of the Heart: Emily Dickinson and the Illogic of Sumptuary Values," *Sulfur* 28 (1991) 134–55.

Keller, Karl. *The Only Kangaroo Among the Beauty: Emily Dickinson and America.* Baltimore: The Johns Hopkins UP, 1979.

Lease, Benjamin. *Emily Dickinson's Readings of Men and Books.* New York: St. Martin's Press, 1990.

Lindberg-Seyersted, Brita. *The Voice of the Poet: Aspects of Style in the Poetry of Emily Dickinson.* Cambridge: Harvard UP, 1968.

Martin, Wendy. *An American Triptych: Anne Bradstreet, Emily Dickinson, Adrienne Rich.* Chapel Hill: U of North Carolina P, 1984.

McGann, Jerome. Introduction. *Black Riders: The Visible Language of Modernism.* Princeton: Princeton UP, 1993.

Miller, Cristanne. *Emily Dickinson: A Poet's Grammar.* Cambridge: Harvard UP, 1987.

Monteiro, George, and Barton Levi St. Armand. "The Experienced Emblem: A Study of the Poetry of Emily Dickinson." *Prospects* 6 (1981): 186–280.

Mudge, Jean McClure. *Emily Dickinson and the Image of Home.* Amherst: U of Massachusetts P, 1975.

Orzeck, Martin and Robert Weisbuch, eds. *Dickinson and Audience.* Ann Arbor: U of Michigan P, 1996.

Patterson, Rebecca. *Emily Dickinson's Imagery.* Ed. Margaret Freeman. Amherst: U of Massachusetts P, 1979.

Paulin, Tom. "Emily Dickinson." *Minotaur, Poetry and the Nation State.* Cambridge: Harvard UP, 1992.

Porter, David T. *The Art of Emily Dickinson's Early Poetry.* Cambridge: Harvard UP, 1966.

Sewall, Richard B., ed. *Emily Dickinson: A Collection of Critical Essays.* Englewood Cliffs: Prentice-Hall, 1963.

Sherwood, William Robert. *Circumference and Circumstance: Stages in the Mind and Art of Emily Dickinson.* New York: Columbia UP, 1968.

Shurr, Willam R., ed. *New Poems of Emily Dickinson.* Chapel Hill: U of North Carolina P, 1993.

Small, Judy Jo. *Positive as Sound: Emily Dickinson's Rhyme.* Athens: U of Georgia P, 1990.

Smith, Martha Nell. *Rowing in Eden: Rereading Emily Dickinson.* Austin: U of Texas P, 1992.

Stocks, Kenneth. *Emily Dickinson and the Modern Consciousness: A Poet of our Time.* New York: St. Martin's, 1988.

Stonum, Gary Lee. *The Dickinson Sublime.* Madison: U of Wisconsin P, 1990.

Tate, Allen. *Collected Essays.* Denver: The Swallow Press, 1932. Scribner's, 1938.

Weisbuch, Robert. *Emily Dickinson's Poetry.* Chicago: U of Chicago P, 1975.

Wells, Henry W. *Introduction to Emily Dickinson.* Chicago: Hendricks House, 1947.

Wilbur, Richard. "Sumptuous Destiny." *Emily Dickinson: Three Views.* Amherst: Amherst College P, 1960.

Wolosky, Shira. *Emily Dickinson: A Voice of War.* New Haven: Yale UP, 1984.

FEMINIST CRITICISM

Barker, Wendy. *Lunacy of Light: Emily Dickinson and the Experience of Metaphor.* Intro. Sandra Gilbert. Carbondale: Southern Illinois UP, 1987.

Bennett, Paula. *Emily Dickinson: Woman Poet.* Iowa City: U of Iowa P, 1991.

Dobson, Joanne. *Dickinson and the Strategies of Reticence: The Woman Writer in Nineteenth-Century America.* Bloomington: Indiana UP, 1989.

Farr, Judith. "Emily Dickinson's 'Engulfing' Play: *Antony and Cleopatra.*" *Tulsa Studies in Women's Literature* 9.1 (1990): 231–50.

Gilbert, Sandra and Susan Gubar. *The Madwoman in the Attic: The Woman Writer and the Nineteenth-Century Literary Imagination.* New Haven: Yale UP, 1979.

Gilbert, Sandra and Susan Gubar, eds. *Shakespeare's Sisters: Feminist Essays on Women Poets.* Bloomington: Indiana UP, 1979.

Juhasz, Suzanne. *"The Undiscovered Continent": Emily Dickinson and the Space of the Mind.* Bloomington: Indiana UP, 1983.

———, Cristanne Miller and Martha Nell Smith. *Comic Power in Emily Dickinson.* Austin: U of Texas P, 1993.

——— and Christanne Miller, eds. *Emily Dickinson: A Celebration for Readers.* New York: Gordon and Breach, 1986. (Conference Proceedings, Claremont College, workshops on individual poems, and plenary sessions)

———, ed. *Feminist Critics Read Emily Dickinson.* Bloomington: Indiana UP, 1983.

Leder, Sharon and Andrea Abbott. *The Language of Exclusion.* New York: Greenwood Press, 1987.

McNeil, Helen. *Emily Dickinson.* London: Virago Press, 1986.

Mossberg, Barbara Antonina Clarke. *Emily Dickinson: When a Writer Is a Daughter.* Bloomington: Indiana UP, 1982.

Pollak, Vivian R. *Dickinson: The Anxiety of Gender.* Ithaca: Cornell UP, 1984.

PURITAN HERITAGE

Doriani, Beth Maclay. *Emily Dickinson: Daughter of Prophecy.* Amherst: U of Massachusetts P, 1996.

St. Armand, Barton Levi. *Emily Dickinson and Her Culture: The Soul's Society.* Cambridge: Cambridge UP, 1984.

PLAY

Luce, William. *The Belle of Amherst: A Play based on the Life of Emily Dickinson.* Boston: Houghton Mifflin, 1976.

MUSIC

Copland, Aaron. *Eight Poems of Emily Dickinson for Voice and Chamber Orchestra.* New York: Boosey and Hawkes, 1970.

PHOTOGRAPHS OF FRIENDS, FAMILY, AND AMHERST

Longsworth, Polly. *The World of Emily Dickinson.* New York: Norton, 1990.

JOURNALS

Two journals are devoted to Dickinson scholarship: *The Emily Dickinson Journal* and *Dickinson Studies*. There are also many articles published about Dickinson in other journals such as *Emerson Society Quarterly* and *American Literature*.

WORLD WIDE WEB SITES

Black, Paul. *440 Emily Dickinson Poems On-line.* <http://www.planet.net/pkrisxle/emily/poemsOnline.html>. Includes links to collections, including University of Maryland's Women's Studies Reading Room. 60 poems are from the 1896 Todd edition.

Gilson, Bill. *Emily Dickinson.* <http://ftp.oit.unc.edu/cheryb/women/Emily-Dickinson-bio.html>. Brief biography.

HarperAudio/Caedmon. <http://www.harperaudio.com/home/index.htm>.

Hollmann, Megan L. *Emily Dickinson Poems.* <http://www.columbia.edu/acis/bartleby/dickinson/>.

Hollmann, Megan L. *Women's Studies Resources.* <http://www.inform.umd.edu/EdRes/Topic/WomensStudies/>.

Kushigian, Nancy and Judith R. Ahronheim. *Poems by Emily Dickinson.* University of Michigan Humanities Text Initiative. <http://www.hti.umich.edu/bin/amv-idx.pl?type=header&id=DickiPoems>. Text taken from 1891 Todd/Higginson edition.

Poetry of Emily Dickinson. 30 Dec. 1995 <http://www.sappho.com/poetry/e_dickin.htm> Brief biography, 3 poems, short bibliography, Lesbian interpretations of the poetry.

Rothberg, Seth. *Edit Poem #585 Yourself.* <http://www.crocker.com/~sethr/lap.html>.

Seidel, Erica, David Shih, and Hilary Vandam. *The Emily Dickinson School: a Hypothetical School designed by three Brown University students, Fall 1993.* <http:/www.netspace.org/users/erica/Ed.dept.homepage.html>.

Sophisticated Shirts. 16 June 1996 <http://www.al.com/shirt/t-shirt.html>. Collection of 50 artistic, scholarly T-shirts and sweatshirts. Order form.

Spear, Lynn. *Emily Dickinson International Society* <http://www.colorado.edu/EDIS/>.

Varrieur, Brian, Barbara Kopeloff, and Jessica Botta. *Alabaster: Archive of Emily Dickinson's Fascicle 26.* <http://www.engl.virginia.edu/~ennc491/frequent/text/home.html>.

Appendix: Documenting Sources

A Guide to MLA
Documentation Style

Documentation is the acknowledgment of information from an outside source that you use in a paper. In general, you should give credit to your sources whenever you quote, paraphrase, summarize, or in any other way incorporate borrowed information or ideas into your work. Not to do so—on purpose or by accident—is to commit **plagiarism,** to appropriate the intellectual property of others. By following accepted conventions of documentation, you not only help avoid plagiarism, but also show your readers that you write with care and precision. In addition, you enable them to distinguish your ideas from those of your sources and, if they wish, to locate and consult the sources you cite.

Not all ideas from your sources need to be documented. You can assume that certain information—facts from encyclopedias, textbooks, newspapers, magazines, and dictionaries, or even from television and radio—is common knowledge. Even if the information is new to you, it need not be documented as long as it is found in several reference sources and as long as you do not use the exact wording of your source. Information that is in dispute or that is the original contribution of a particular person, however, *must* be documented. You need not, for example, document the fact that Arthur Miller's *Death of a Salesman* was first performed in 1949 or that it won a Pulitzer Prize for drama. (You could find this information in any current encyclopedia.) You would, however, have to document a critic's interpretation of a performance or a scholar's analysis of an early draft of the play, even if you do not use your source's exact words.

Students of literature use the documentation style recommended by the Modern Language Association of America (MLA), a professional organization of more than twenty-five thousand teachers and students of English and other languages. This method of documentation, the one that you should use any time you write a literature paper, has three components: *parenthetical references in the text, a list of works cited,* and *explanatory notes.*

Parenthetical References in the Text

MLA documentation uses references inserted in parentheses within the text that refer to an alphabetical list of works cited at the end of the paper. A typical **parenthetical reference** consists of the author's last name and a page number.

> Gwendolyn Brooks uses the sonnet form to create poems that have a wide social and aesthetic range (Williams 972).

If you use more than one source by the same author, include a shortened title in the parenthetical reference. In the following entry, "Brooks's Way" is a shortened form of the complete title of the article "Gwendolyn Brooks's Way with the Sonnet."

> Brooks not only knows Shakespeare, Spenser, and Milton, but she also knows the full range of African-American poetry (Williams, "Brooks's Way" 972).

If you mention the author's name or the title of the work in your paper, only a page reference is necessary.

> According to Gladys Margaret Williams in "Gwendolyn Brooks's Way with the Sonnet," Brooks combines a sensitivity to poetic forms with a depth of emotion appropriate for her subject matter (972–73).

Keep in mind that you use different punctuation for parenthetical references used with *paraphrases and summaries,* with *direct quotations run in with the text,* and with *quotations of more than four lines.*

Paraphrases and Summaries

Place the parenthetical reference after the last word of the sentence and before the final punctuation:

> In her works Brooks combines the pessimism of Modernist poetry with the optimism of the Harlem Renaissance (Smith 978).

Direct quotations run in with the text

Place the parenthetical reference after the quotation marks and before the final punctuation:

> According to Gary Smith, Brooks's <u>A Street in Bronzeville</u> "conveys the primacy of suffering in the lives of poor Black women" (980).

> According to Gary Smith, the poems in <u>A Street in Bronzeville</u>, "served notice that Brooks had learned her craft . . ." (978).

> Along with Thompson we must ask, "Why did it take so long for critics to acknowledge that Gwendolyn Brooks is an important voice in twentieth-century American poetry?" (123)

Quotations set off from the text

Omit the quotation marks and place the parenthetical reference one space after the final punctuation.

> For Gary Smith, the identity of Brooks's African-American women is inextricably linked with their sense of race and poverty:
>> For Brooks, unlike the Renaissance poets, the victimization of poor Black women becomes not simply a minor chord but a predominant theme of <u>A Street in Bronzeville</u>. Few, if any, of her female characters are able to free themselves from a web of poverty that threatens to strangle their lives. (980)

[Quotations of more than four lines are indented ten spaces (or one inch) from the margin and are not enclosed within quotation marks. The first line of a single paragraph of quoted material is not indented further. If you quote two or more paragraphs, indent the first line of each paragraph three additional spaces (one-quarter inch).]

SAMPLE REFERENCES

The following formats are used for parenthetical references to various kinds of sources used in papers about literature. (Keep in mind that the parenthetical reference contains just enough information to enable readers to find the source in the list of works cited at the end of the paper.)

An entire work

August Wilson's play <u>Fences</u> treats many themes frequently expressed in modern drama.

[When citing an entire work, state the name of the author in your paper instead of in a parenthetical reference.]

A work by two or three authors

Myths cut across boundaries and cultural spheres and reappear in strikingly similar forms from country to country (Feldman and Richardson 124).

The effect of a work of literature depends on the audience's predispositions that derive from membership in various social groups (Hovland, Janis, and Kelley 87).

A work by more than three authors

Hawthorne's short stories frequently use a combination of allegorical and symbolic methods (Guerin et al. 91).

[The abbreviation *et al.* is Latin for "and others."]

A work in an anthology

In his essay "Flat and Round Characters" E. M. Forster distinguishes between one-dimensional characters and those that are well developed (Stevick 223-31).

[The parenthetical reference cites the anthology (edited by Stevick) that contains Forster's essay; full information about the anthology appears in the list of works cited.]

A work with volume and page numbers

In 1961 one of Albee's plays, <u>The Zoo Story</u>, was
finally performed in America (Eagleton 2:17).

An indirect source

Wagner observed that myth and history stood before
him "with opposing claims" (qtd. in Winkler 10).

[The abbreviation *qtd. in* (quoted in) indicates that the quoted material was
not taken from the original source.]

A play or poem with numbered lines

"Give thy thoughts no tongue," says Polonius,
"Nor any unproportioned thought his act"
(<u>Ham</u>. 1.3.59–60).

[The parentheses contain the act, scene, and line numbers, separated by periods. When included in parenthetical references, titles of the books of the Bible and well-known literary works are often abbreviated—*Gen.* for *Genesis* and *Ado* for *Much Ado about Nothing,* for example.]

"I muse my life-long hate, and without flinch / I
bear it nobly as I live my part," says Claude McKay
in his bitterly ironic poem "The White City" (3–4).

[Notice that a slash [/] is used to separate lines of poetry run in with the text. The parenthetical reference cites the lines quoted.]

The List of Works Cited

Parenthetical references refer to a **list of works cited** that includes all the sources you refer to in your paper. (If your list includes all the works consulted, whether you cite them or not, use the title *Works Consulted.*) Begin the works cited list on a new page, continuing the page numbers of the paper. For example, if the text of the paper ends on page six, the works cited section will begin on page seven.

Center the title *Works Cited* one inch from the top of the page. Arrange entries alphabetically, according to the last name of each author (or the first word of the title if the author is unknown). Articles—*a, an,* and *the*—at the beginning of a title are not considered first words. Thus, *A Handbook of Critical Approaches to Literature* would be alphabetized under *H.* In order to conserve space, publishers' names are abbreviated—for example, *Harcourt* for Harcourt Brace College Publishers. Double-space the entire works cited list between and within entries. Begin typing each entry at the left margin, and indent subsequent lines five spaces or one-half inch. The entry itself generally has three divisions—author, title, and publishing information—separated by periods.*

A book by a single author

Kingston, Maxine Hong. <u>The Woman Warrior: Memoirs of a Girlhood among Ghosts</u>. New York: Knopf, 1976.

A book by two or three authors

Feldman, Burton, and Robert D. Richardson. <u>The Rise of Modern Mythology</u>. Bloomington: Indiana UP, 1972.

[Notice that only the *first* author's name is in reverse order.]

A book by more than three authors

Guerin, Wilfred, et al., eds. <u>A Handbook of Critical Approaches to Literature</u>. 3rd. ed. New York: Harper, 1992.

[Instead of using *et al.,* you may list all the authors' names in the order in which they appear on the title page.]

Two or more works by the same author

Novoa, Juan-Bruce. <u>Chicano Authors: Inquiry by Interview</u>. Austin: U of Texas P, 1980.

---

* The fourth edition of the *MLA Handbook for Writers of Research Papers* (1995) shows a single space after all end punctuation.

```
---. "Themes in Rudolfo Anaya's Work." Address
     given at New Mexico State University, Las
     Cruces. 11 Apr. 1987.
```

[List two or more works by the same author in alphabetical order by title. Include the author's full name in the first entry; use three unspaced hyphens followed by a period to take the place of the author's name in second and subsequent entries.]

An edited book

```
Oosthuizen, Ann, ed. Sometimes When It Rains: Writ-
     ings by South African Women. New York: Pandora,
     1987.
```

[Note that the abbreviation *ed.* stands for *editor.*]

A book with a volume number

```
Eagleton, T. Allston. A History of the New York
     Stage. Vol. 2. Englewood Cliffs: Prentice.
     1987.
```

[All three volumes have the same title.]

```
Durant, Will, and Ariel Durant. The Age of Napoleon:
     A History of European Civilization from 1789 to
     1815. New York: Simon, 1975.
```

[Each volume has a different title, so you may cite an individual book without referring to the other volumes.]

A short story, poem, or play in a collection of the author's work

```
Gordimer, Nadine. "Once upon a Time." "Jump" and
     Other Stories. New York: Farrar, 1991. 23-30.
```

A short story in an anthology

```
Salinas, Marta. "The Scholarship Jacket." Nosotros:
     Latina Literature Today. Ed. Maria del Carmen
```

```
Boza, Beverly Silva, and Carmen Valle. Bingham-
    ton: Bilingual, 1986. 68-70.
```

[The inclusive page numbers follow the year of publication. Note that here the abbreviation *Ed.* stands for *Edited by*.]

A poem in an anthology

```
Simmerman, Jim. "Child's Grave, Hale County, Ala-
    bama." The Pushcart Prize, X: Best of the Small
    Presses. Ed. Bill Henderson. New York: Penguin,
    1986. 198-99.
```

A play in an anthology

```
Hughes, Langston. Mother and Child. Black Drama An-
    thology. Ed. Woodie King and Ron Miller. New
    York: NAL, 1986.399-406.
```

An article in an anthology

```
Forster, E. M. "Flat and Round Characters." The The-
    ory of the Novel. Ed. Philip Stevick. New York:
    Free, 1980. 223-31.
```

More than one selection from the same anthology

If you are using more than one selection from an anthology, cite the anthology in one entry. In addition, list each individual selection separately, including the author and title of the selection, the anthology editor's last name, and the inclusive page numbers.

```
Kirszner, Laurie G., and Stephen R. Mandell, eds.
    Literature: Reading, Reacting, Writing. 3rd ed.
    Fort Worth: Harcourt, 1997.
Rich, Adrienne. "Diving into the Wreck." Kirszner
    and Mandell 874-76.
```

A translation

```
Carpentier, Alejo. Reasons of State. Trans. Francis
    Partridge. New York: Norton, 1976.
```

An article in a journal with continuous pagination in each issue

> LeGuin, Ursula K. "American Science Fiction and the
>   Other." Science Fiction Studies 2 (1975):
>   208-10.

An article with separate pagination in each issue

> Grossman, Robert. "The Grotesque in Faulkner's
>   'A Rose for Emily.'" Mosaic 20.3 (1987): 40-55.

[20.3 signifies volume 20, issue 3.]

An article in a magazine

> Milosz, Czeslaw. "A Lecture." New Yorker 22 June
>   1992: 32.
> "Solzhenitsyn: An Artist Becomes an Exile." Time
>   25 Feb. 1974: 34+.

[34+ indicates that the article appears on pages that are not consecutive; in this case the article begins on page 34 and then continues on page 37. An article with no listed author is entered by title on the works cited list.]

An article in a daily newspaper

> Oates, Joyce Carol. "When Characters from the Page
>   Are Made Flesh on the Screen." New York Times
>   23 Mar. 1986, late ed.: C1+.

[C1+ indicates that the article begins on page 1 of Section C and continues on a subsequent page.]

An article in a reference book

> "Dance Theatre of Harlem." The New Encyclopaedia
>   Britannica: Micropaedia. 15th ed. 1987.

[You do not need to include publication information for well-known reference books.]

> Grimstead, David. "Fuller, Margaret Sarah." Encyclo-
>   pedia of American Biography. Ed. John A. Gar-
>   raty. New York: Harper, 1974.

[You must include publication information when citing reference books that are not well known.]

A CD-ROM: Entry with a print version

```
Zurbach, Kate. "The Linguistic Roots of Three
     Terms." Linguistic Quarterly 37 (1994): 12-47.
     Infotrac: Magazine Index Plus. CD-ROM. Informa-
     tion Access. Jan. 1996.
```

[When you cite information with a print version from a CD-ROM, include the publication information, the underlined title of the database (Infotrac: Magazine Index Plus), the publication medium (CD-ROM), the name of the company that produced the CD-ROM (Information Access), and the electronic publication date.]

A CD-ROM: Entry with no print version

```
"Surrealism." Encarta 1996. CD-ROM. Redmond: Micro-
     soft, 1996.
```

[If you are citing a part of a work, include the title in quotation marks.]

```
A Music Lover's Multimedia Guide to Beethoven's 5th.
     CD-ROM. Spring Valley: Interactive, 1993.
```

[If you are citing an entire work, include the underlined title.]

An online source: Entry with a print version

```
Dekoven, Marianne. "Utopias Limited: Post-sixties
     and Postmodern American Fiction." Modern Fic-
     tion Studies 41.1 (Spring 1995): 121-34.
     17 Mar. 1996 <http://muse.jhu.edu/journals/
     MFS/v041/41.1 dekoven.html>.
```

[When you cite information with a print version from an online source, include the publication information for the printed source, the number of pages or the number of paragraphs (if available), and the date of access. Include the electronic address, or URL, in angle brackets. Information from a commercial computer service—America Online, Prodigy, and CompuServ, for example—will not have an electronic address.]

O'Hara, Sandra. "Reexamining the Canon." <u>Time</u> 13 May
    1994: 27. America Online. 22 Aug. 1994.

An online source: Entry with no print version

"Romanticism." <u>Academic American Encyclopedia</u>. Sept.
    1996. Prodigy. 6 Nov. 1995.

[This entry shows that the material was accessed on November 6, 1996.]

An online source: Public Posting

Peters, Olaf. "Studying English through German."
    Online posting. 29 Feb. 1996. Foreign Language
    Forum, Multi Language Section. CompuServe.
    15 Mar. 1996.
Gilford, Mary. "Dog Heroes in Children's Litera-
    ture." 4 Oct. 1996. 23 Mar. 1996 <News:
    alt.animals.dogs>.

[**WARNING:** Using information from online forums and newsgroups is
risky. Contributors are not necessarily experts, and frequently they are
incorrect and misinformed. Unless you can be certain that the informa-
tion you are receiving from these sources is reliable, do not use it in your
papers.]

An online source: Electronic Text

Twain, Mark. <u>The Adventures of Huckleberry Finn</u>.
    From <u>The Writing of Mark Twain</u>. Vol. 13.
    New York: Harper, 1970. <u>Wiretap.spies</u>.
    13 Jan. 1996 <http.//www.sci.dixie.edu/
    DixieCollege/Ebooks/huckfin.html>.

[This electronic text was originally published by Harper. The name of the
repository for the electronic edition is Wiretap.spies. (underlined)]

An online source: E-Mail

Adkins, Camille. E-Mail to the author. 8 June 1995.

An interview

```
Brooks, Gwendolyn. "Interviews." Triquarterly 60
     (1984): 405-10.
```

A lecture or address

```
Novoa, Juan-Bruce. "Themes in Rudolfo Anaya's Work."
     New Mexico State University, Las Cruces,
     11 Apr. 1987.
```

A film or videocassette

```
"A Worn Path." By Eudora Welty. Dir. John Reid and
     Claudia Velasco. Perf. Cora Lee Day and Con-
     chita Ferrell. Videocassette. Harcourt, 1994.
```

[In addition to the title, the director, and the year, include other pertinent information such as the principal performers.]

Explanatory Notes

Explanatory notes, indicated by a superscript (a raised number) in the text, may be used to cite several sources at once or to provide commentary or explanations that do not fit smoothly into your paper. The full text of these notes appears on the first numbered page following the last page of the paper. (If your paper has no explanatory notes, the works cited page follows the last page of the paper.) Like works cited entries, explanatory notes are double-spaced within and between entries. However, the first line of each explanatory note is indented five spaces (or one-half inch), with subsequent lines flush with the left-hand margin.

TO CITE SEVERAL SOURCES

In the paper

```
Surprising as it may seem, there have been many
attempts to define literature.[1]
```

In the note

    [1] For an overview of critical opinion, see Arnold 72; Eagleton 1–2; Howe 43–44; and Abrams 232–34.

TO PROVIDE EXPLANATIONS

In the paper

    In recent years Gothic novels have achieved great popularity.[3]

In the note

    [3] Gothic novels, works written in imitation of medieval romances, originally relied on supernatural occurrences. They flourished in the late eighteenth and early nineteenth centuries.

Credits

Suzanne Juhasz
"The Wayward Nun beneath the Hill" from *Feminist Critics Read Emily Dickinson*
by Suzanne Juhasz. Reprinted by permission of Indiana University Press.

Richard B. Sewall
Excerpt from *The Life of Emily Dickinson* by Richard B. Sewall. Copyright © 1974
by Richard B. Sewall. Reprinted by permission of Farrar, Straus & Giroux, Inc.

Judy Jo Small
Excerpt from "A Musical Aesthetic" in *Positive as Sound: Emily Dickinson's Rhyme*
by Judy Jo Small. Reprinted by permission of The University of Georgia Press.

Allen Tate
"Emily Dickinson" by Allen Tate from *Collected Essays,* pp. 199–213. Reprinted by
permission of Mrs. Helen Tate.

Henry W. Wells
"Romantic Sensibility" by Henry W. Wells from *Introduction to Emily Dickinson.*
Copyright 1947. Reprinted by permission of Hendricks House, Putney, VT
05346.

STUDENT ESSAY

Rachel Lavery
"The Musicality of Emily Dickinson's Poetry" by Rachel Lavery. Reprinted by
permission.